Internet Marketing for the Small Business Owner

A Handbook and Reference Guide for the Small or Local Business Owner

By Tad and Tricia Stephens

Legal Notice:

This book is copyright protected. This is only for personal use. You cannot amend, distribute, sell, use, quote or paraphrase any part or the content within this book without the consent of the author or copyright owner. Legal action will be pursued if this is breached.

Disclaimer Notice:

Please note the information contained within this document is for educational purposes only.

Every attempt has been made to provide accurate, up to date and reliable complete information however no warranties of any kind are expressed or implied. Readers acknowledge that the author is not engaging in rendering legal, financial or professional advice.

By reading any document, the reader agrees that under no circumstances are we responsible for any losses, direct or indirect, financial or otherwise, which are incurred as a result of use of the information contained within this document, including – but not limited to errors, omissions, or inaccuracies.

All marks and trademarks are the property of their respective owners.

Table of Contents

<u>Preface</u>

You're Busy, We Understand.

In 2002 my wife and I decided to create a website to sell Continuing Professional Education (CPE) to Certified Public Accountants (CPAs). We had never done anything like that before and in 2004 we launched <u>www.cpethink.com</u>. Ten years later we have a growing online business and are a Tier 1 CPE provider nationwide and worldwide. We provide CPE to Fortune 500 firms, staff accountants, and all sizes of accounting firms – all online.

After developing the website we had to figure out how to market it, we had never done that either. We outsourced or contracted out our marketing three separate times and each time our sales went down. So we learned how, on our own, and now we outsource some and do some in house, just took us a while to learn how and figure which to do what with.

What I wanted but never found was a course, guide book, reference guide, anything to let me know the marketing environment, marketing channels available and up and coming. Something I could keep on my desk to lookup a technology or channel before getting ready to take a call from a salesperson wanting to sell me that technology. But also something that would give me the 50,000 foot view to know what was out there and how the different channels worked together or not. I knew I needed Internet Marketing, I just didn't know what kind or how much. What you are reading is all of that in a single place.

Since 2004 I have taken in person courses, read countless whitepapers and articles, taken a multitude of online courses, and bought hundreds of online business marketing "opportunities". Some worked, some didn't but I almost always took away something to use. I had to figure this out and was as determined then as I am today.

That and ten years of marketing online taught me the Internet Marketing "business" but I still had a big problem since I wanted to write a book. I am a terrible writer. Luckily my wife is not. So again we decided to do something we had not done before, but as you have probably figured out by now that rarely stops us.

This book is technical and it is not technical. It is concise yet detailed. It is written for the business owner or manager (or both) that knows they need to market or thinks they do but does not have time to take or read hundreds of course, whitepapers, articles, business marketing opportunities, etc. If you are that person (or a close relative or facsimile) keep reading.

This book is also written to be used as a whole and as individual chapters. Want a quick update on Facebook Marketing? Then just read the chapter on Facebook. Want to know more on Search Engine Optimization? Then just read that chapter. Want to know Internet Marketing from a broad perspective? Then read the book from cover to cover.

The world of Internet Marketing is ever changing. Consider the growth of Facebook and that Google changes it's algorithm on average twice a day. Because of that we plan on updating this book at least once a year, possibly more frequently depending on what changes. In between updates we will post new information and updates on our website at http://www.mediamarketexperts.com/category /internet-marketing-book-updates/. Please stop by anytime and get the latest!

Still not convinced? Buy the book, if you haven't already, and if you think it is not worth twice what you paid for it send us an Email at service@mediamarketexperts.com and we will refund your full purchase price via PayPal (sorry, no checks).

And finally we started another business (starting to see a pattern?) so others small businesses like us would not have to go through what we did to learn and implement all of this. We do Internet Marketing consulting and fulfillment to generate leads and convert those leads into sales. Stop by and see us at www.mediamarketexperts.com and let us know what you think.

And most of all we truly hope the book helps.

Sincerely,

Tad Stephens – Too stubborn to stop and get a real job.

P.S. Connect with me on LinkedIn - http://www.linkedin.com/in/tadstephens

Section 1: The Problem

The Brave New World

Once upon a time, it was a fairly simple task to get the word out about your business. You could reach a huge swath of the population with relatively little complication by crafting a good sign for your storefront, distributing fliers throughout the neighborhood, having a grand opening sale and maybe even taking out a spot on the radio or on television.

For some businesses, it still is that simple. The first rule of marketing, after all, is *to go where your audience is already gathered.* If your business primarily services people that don't gather, socialize or search on the Internet, this book isn't for you.

However, for 2014 and after –it's becoming increasingly difficult to find any group of people that *doesn't* use the Internet. For the vast majority of small brick-and-mortar businesses, it not only makes sense to market on the Internet, *it's necessary for the survival of your enterprise.*

Consider this: The Internet marketing ship is quickly leaving the harbor. With every year that goes by, marketing online becomes more ubiquitous, more sophisticated, and continues to diminish the returns you would get from offline advertising. According to Internet World Stats, one-third of the world's population is online as of 2012, and almost 80% of the United States is, as well. And according to iJailbreak, there are now more people in the world with cell phones than toothbrushes. People spend a lot of time Googling answers to their questions, watching videos on YouTube and sharing pictures and stories on Facebook – and that time is taking away from the amount they used to spend on legacy media like television and radio. The online audience continues to grow every year, and Internet marketing only continues to get more and more effective as time goes on.

It's a brave new world! However, a lot of businesses just keep doing things the way they have been for the last decade (or more) because they don't understand how easy – and profitable – it is to get started with Internet marketing. They don't understand that the Web has completely revolutionized commerce, from trade on a global scale down to the smallest mom-and-pop shop.

What is Internet Marketing?

Internet Marketing includes indirect marketing elements, direct response marketing, and uses many different processes, procedures and platforms, from search engines to banner advertisements to social media. Simply defined, it's anything a business does online in order to attract new business, retain current customers and develop its brand.

Why Should You Market Online?

There are many benefits of Internet marketing over traditional marketing:

- Reach. Because the Internet is global, that means your business can be, as well. It used to be that you had to be a huge, international corporation in order to business all around the world. Now, anyone with a WiFi connection or a smartphone can access potential customers anywhere in the world without breaking the bank on a big marketing budget. If you are not global but local, consider this: You can potentially reach everyone in your geographic area that has a smartphone, tablet, or personal computer of any flavor.

- Scope. Because you can reach so many people in so many different ways, you can offer people a wider range of products and services. Internet marketing includes (among other things) information management, customer service, sales and public relations. As new technologies become available, the scope of your potential only grows.

- Demographics and Targeting. As a group, Internet users have greater buying power, because they tend to skew – demographically speaking – toward the middle class. But it's not all about buying power. Internet users also organize themselves into niches, making it easier to access and target small, focused groups of consumers who have organized around a single interest or industry.

- Interactivity. The point of traditional marketing is to get your brand's message in front of people's eyes. However, Internet marketing creates a two-way road between your business and your customers, allowing you to be more responsive and dynamic in your service interactions.

- Immediacy. Because of the interactive nature of the Web, it's now easier than ever to immediately move a customer through the steps of your marketing funnel. Imagine a customer viewing a commercial on television when they're sitting at home, or reading an advertisement in a magazine when they're at the salon. They have learned about a product, but there are additional steps to acquiring it. With Internet marketing, you can learn about a product or service and, just a few clicks later, have already purchased it – and this can happen 24 hours a day, 7 days a week, regardless of whether your store is open.

- Adaptivity. Marketing requires regular, consistent measurement of metrics in order to determine whether you're even getting a return on your investment. Internet marketing allows continuous tracking of these metrics, and allows you to dynamically change your tactics mid-campaign any time you see the need to adapt to your customer's wants and needs.

The World Wide Web for Local Businesses

Because the Internet is such a worldwide phenomenon, many local businesses believe that Internet marketing won't benefit them in the same way it does a multinational corporation with a global reach. After all, the local hardware store doesn't advertise during the Superbowl!

We might amend an old bumper sticker saying in order to describe this concept best: Think globally, sell locally. As it turns out, there are many options available online for local geographical targeting that allow a small business to only target folks in their area who are searching for a product related to their own. According to Search Engine Land, 43% of Google searches are location specific, and Google has a service called Google Places with over 4 million listings for small businesses. On average, 95% of businesses that use sites like Groupon or other hyper-local daily deals services are satisfied with their experience and would use it again. And many small businesses have greatly expanded their customer base – and customer satisfaction – by employing social media marketing on platforms like Facebook, Twitter and Pinterest.

There are many other forms of Internet Marketing – many of which are covered in this book – and more are invented all the time. Promoting your business online not only allows you to reach customers that are gathering online and aren't as susceptible to traditional marketing; it also allows you to generate interest in your business outside your locality, expanding your business's reach.

In short, in this brave new Internet-enabled world of ours, the rules of business have dramatically changed. Your customers are out there, waiting for you to reach them. All it takes is a willingness to do it.

Section 2: The Alternatives

Alternatives: Building a Website

All right – you know you've got to build a website in order to get started with Internet marketing. But even the most web-savvy business owner has to start somewhere. And where is that?

It all starts by creating a winning website within a tailored budget. You're not a huge multinational corporation who can afford to spend millions on a website – you need a functional, aesthetic, effective website to lend you credibility and enable your Internet marketing strategy, and you need to do it without breaking the bank.

No problem! There is no reason a website should cost more than you can afford. Let's dive into the details.

The Theory

You need a website for many reasons. It's the focal point of your Internet marketing strategy, sure. But it's also the best tool available to businesses in the Digital Age to help influence consumers. A website is crucial to your business's visibility – a shop window, of sorts, that can entice people to come in and buy.

In this day and age, it gives off a bad impression if you don't have a website. It would be akin to not having a telephone number or an address. It's a necessary investment in the success of your business.

That said, it's not just a window dressing, either. The primary purpose of having a website is to get traffic. You want people's eyes on your product or service – after all, why have an awesome business if no one has any way of finding out about it?

Do It Yourself (DIY) Website Construction

Like most small business owners, you're probably on a tight budget, and it might be out of your reach to hire a professional Web developer. However, you have to compare the costs of hiring an expert against the costs of spending a lot of your time learning, building and maintaining your own site. It's easy to get sticker shock when considering high up-front costs, but don't make the mistake of letting the opportunity costs of DIY website construction empty your pockets. While you're developing your site, you're not developing your business!

If you decide to create your own site, the #1 platform for that is called <u>WordPress</u>. It's fast, relatively easy, requires little to no knowledge of HTML, and comes with thousands of prepackaged themes (site design templates) you can use that have already been constructed with user experience in mind. To do anything advanced, such as e-commerce, you'll have to learn how to create and maintain web content, however.

Two other platforms you can consider are <u>Blogger</u> and <u>Tumblr</u>. They're both highly easy and intuitive; however, hosting a site with either of these sometimes looks unprofessional to prospective clients. Building a site on either Blogger or Tumblr should only ever be used as a stepping stone to a future web page, especially because neither platform has useful, intuitive capabilities for hosting advanced functionalities.

Hiring A Developer

Why should you decide to spend money on a developer rather than doing it yourself? Web design is a discipline that blends art and science, and takes a long time to become an expert in. If you want to make sure customers have a great first impression of your business and can intuitively use every feature of your site, all while looking great, it can be a steep learning curve – and you still might not have the best website possible. You have to decide whether your potential return on investment will be high enough to justify hiring a web designer or a design firm.

If you decide to go this route, the number one key to guiding the designer's work is in setting objectives to make your website purposeful. What is the purpose of your website? Raising awareness? Generating leads? Closing sales? If you want to sell your product or service online, you'll need e-commerce functionality, with a "shopping cart" and secure payment systems. If you're only using your site for marketing, you need to make sure you've got plenty of ways for folks to contact you so they can set up their desired offline transactions – Email, phone numbers, physical address and even live chat windows are excellent facilitators.

Even if you've hired a professional to create your site, you're going to need to learn how to maintain and edit it so you can keep it fresh and current. Not only is the "freshness" of a website (how often it is updated) imperative to potential customers (no one likes to see a website that hasn't been updated in a year,) it's also crucial to your search engine rankings. Of course, we'll cover more about that in the chapter on search engines.

You've also got to be sure to test your site regularly. Is it compatible for all browsers, including Internet Explorer, Firefox, Opera, Safari and Chrome? Is it optimized for mobile devices like smartphones and tablets? Your designer should handle these considerations, but it's up to you to inspect what you expect.

What Makes A Good Website?

According to Netcraft.com, as of 2012, there were over 600 million websites on the Internet. That should tell you it's a game that anyone can play. But it's not a game that everyone plays well! Here are six essential elements of a good website:

1. The website is built around a purpose. A good website meets the purpose of the site, and isn't overly broad or lacking focus in its approach. A website that tries to do too much just ends up with a muddled, disorganized design, that confuses readers. If the readers are confused, they're not confident in your business – and they're not going to do business with you. Remember the marketing adage; a confused reader never buys. When it comes to websites, they don't always have to be simple, but they do have to be elegant, intuitive, and able to communicate effectively and quickly.

2. The website has credible, authoritative information that provides value to users. This is a measure of quality that exists independent of the purpose of the website. People surf the Internet for content, and if your content isn't useful and credible, people won't find value in it and won't use your site. Plain and simple. Likewise, your content needs to

be up-to-date, copyedited and free of typographical errors and complete. Too many sites try to hire freelance "writers" for bottom-of-the-barrel fees that lack credentials or experience; those sites end up with ugly, ineffective web copy that alienates or confuses their visitors. If you're not a natural writer, you may need to hire a professional to write your web copy and content for you. We'll cover more on what great content looks like in the chapter on content marketing a little later in the book.

3. The website is easy to use and easy to access. You can build the most elegant, purposeful site on the Web, with the most valuable, credible information available, and if people can't use it, all of that effort was for naught. This principle comes back to simplicity. If your web pages are disorganized, if there are too many links (or if the links are broken and don't lead anywhere) or if the information doesn't flow in a natural, organic way, you're going to turn people off from using your site, and people that can't use your site definitely won't give you their business.

4. The website is well-designed. Web design – both in terms of user experience and graphics – is key to establishing your credibility. A website should use small graphics that don't take a long time to load and that always fit the content. Similarly, the graphics shouldn't blink, move or flash or do anything else – these grab people's attention, but Web users hate them because they distract from a page's content and remind them too much of the pushy, overbearing advertisements many marketers use. The layout of the site should be as simple as possible – think the three-column layout used in newspapers, or the standard blog format you know and love. When people recognize the layout, they're comfortable with it, and more likely to engage with your content. It's also important to use white space correctly, ensure that headlines use a serif (Sometimes Called With Feet As This Is) font and body text uses a sans-serif (without feet) font, and that you never use more than three standard font families on a page.

5. The website's ads are under control. Whether you're letting another business advertise on your site (if you're in the content business, for instance) or you're advertising your own call-to-action, don't be greedy with people's attention. People usually don't go to websites with the intention of buying something – they're there to consume content and research a buying decision. This is a slow, organic process that you need to respect. If you overwhelm the content of the page with ads or intrusive calls-to-action, you'll drive users away. Instead, treat your advertisements the way you would any other image (except calls-to-action, which should be prominent without being intrusive.)

6. The website has a good domain name. The websites people return to are the websites people can remember. Not everyone remembers to bookmark sites they're interested in returning to, because not everyone is sure they're going to be interested in coming back to it the first time they visit! Having an overly complicated domain name (or one hosted on a free server, such as the

aforementioned Tumblr) makes it difficult for people to remember your site, and also conveys an image of unprofessionalism. Also, be careful about having a single domain name that ends in .net, .co or anything besides .com. Most folks only remember .com as an ending, and won't remember how to access your page again in the future. Lastly, there are many hosting companies and domain name registries available on the web, and they vary in their price and usefulness. But remember that when you're selecting a service to host your site and register your name, you get what you pay for. You want to select a hosting company that can guarantee that your site won't go down for long periods of time – because every moment your content isn't available to folks is every moment your site isn't driving traffic or sales to your business.

Step-By-Step

There isn't a magic formula you can follow to make a great website, but there is a simple, step-by-step list of actions you can take to get one up and going.

1. Name your site. Ideally, this should be the same name as your business. If you can't get that domain name for any reason, try to pick something generic that relates to your product or service, so that people can draw natural, easy connections between your site and your business.

2. Register your domain and secure site hosting. Many companies do both domain registry and web hosting; as we mentioned before, you get what you pay for! So don't just go for the bottom of the barrel when it comes to price.

3. Choose your theme (a predefined website template). The theme determines the usability, feel and aesthetics of your site. WordPress has thousands of these you can use for free (or purchase for a small fee) that will give you endless customization options for your website. These are helpful for those of us that aren't computer scientists, because it gets a web page up

and running without all the hours it would take to learn to code and design a site. Using a theme also lets you adjust interface, colors, functionality and more – so you can optimize your users' experience.

4. Get a logo. Your business should already have a logo, but if it doesn't, you need one quick. If you don't have training in graphic design, don't design it yourself; a bad logo can actually harm your business by undermining your credibility with consumers. Sites like Elance and ODesk are a good resource for finding graphic designers that will deliver you a professional, aesthetic logo that will strengthen your brand.

5. Build the core functionality of the site. If you're trying to sell online, this is the part where you build e-commerce functionality. If you're using the site for content marketing, start creating and posting content! And if you're primarily concerned with an informational page to help customers find your offline business, ensure your home page has everything a consumer

needs to make a decision about whether (and how) to do business with you.

Alternatives: Search Engine Optimization

According to StatisticBrain, people use search engines billions of times per day (yes billions with a "B"). Sites like Google, Bing and Yahoo! are the primary drivers of nearly all Web traffic.

When folks are out searching the Internet, they usually have a question they need answered or a problem they need solved, and you want your business to be found by potential customers who are looking for the products or services that you offer! In order to do that, you'll need to understand how search engines work. You want to construct your web pages and website in a manner that makes it as easy as possible for search engines to connect people with your business.

What Are Search Engines?

The dictionary definition is: "A program for the retrieval of data from a database or network, especially the Internet." But you already knew that. A search engine is a simple program – usually a website – where you type in a question or problem or phrase you want more information on, and then it delivers you results that are relative to your search. There are four search platforms that are important to Internet Marketing: Facebook, LinkedIn, Bing and (most crucially) Google. As you gain experience with Internet marketing, you'll want to expand your focus to all of these platforms, but for now, Google is the most important search engine you need to learn about.

Google

With 67% of the market share, this is the search engine you most likely use on a daily basis, and the one you need to know the most about as you begin marketing on the Internet. Google was started back in the late 1990s as a simple search engine, and has grown into one of the largest companies in the world, with a reach that pervades nearly every aspect of the Internet. Though it has expanded into many other business segments like maps, social media and Email, the core of Google still revolves around its search feature. Going forward, we'll focus on Google, because the bulk of your marketing efforts should be geared toward this company's platforms.

How Do Search Engines Work?

The Internet is incredibly huge – there are billions upon billions of pages out there – so search engines organize and catalog them (called indexing) to help other folks find what they're looking for.

Crawling

There is a kind of program that search engines run, often called a "crawler", "bot", or "spider" that moves from URL to URL on as many web pages as they can find, gathering information on their content and metadata (data about the data on your page). The spiders collect information from hundreds of signals on a web page and report back to the search engine.

Indexing

After spiders have reported back, Google parses the information they've collected and indexes web pages based on their potential relevance to certain topics or phrases.

The Key Difference

The terms "crawling" or "spidering" and "indexing" are sometimes used interchangeably, but they're different things. Just because a site has been crawled doesn't mean it's been indexed. Essentially, Google learns about URLs out in the sphere of the Web and schedules them to be crawled – once they're crawled, Google can figure out how to organize those URLs in terms of relevance, which is the act of indexing. Google may decide to ignore a page after it has been crawled in which case that page would not be indexed.

Types of Searches

The classic mode of searching is through text – a user types in something they're looking for, and Google returns a list of links they can click on that are likely relevant.

There have been some major changes to the way Google handles text searches, which we'll cover shortly. Suffice it to say (for now) that Google no longer simply reads what the user has typed into the box – it actually attempts to figure out what the user intends.

The world is changing, and people are accessing search engines in very different ways than they did when Google was first launched back in 1998. Google's most recent algorithm, known as Hummingbird (we'll cover that shortly) was launched to better accommodate different kinds of search, like:

- Voice. Most smartphones have a feature where you can input text by voice. However, people speak differently than they write, and Google had to account for this when reconfiguring their algorithm. They are also competing with Apple's app, called Siri, a kind of virtual assistant that one speaks to in order to engage, and who responds with search results, weather, local business information and more – also by voice. And have you noticed the microphone in the Google Search box?

- Visual. You've probably heard of Google Glass, the newest groundbreaking invention from the search giant. It's a set of glasses one wears that gives them a Heads-Up Display of information as an overlay on the real world they're perceiving. They received a patent for a "Gaze Tracking System" which tracks eye movement and pupil dilation. The Hummingbird update builds more semantic, organic understanding into Google search to be able to process data like where users are looking, and what kind of emotional response they are having.

The Algorithm

Google has several patented algorithms that determine how high a web page will appear on their search results page. One of the major reasons that Google established such dominance in the search market is because of the ingenuity of these algorithms – they collects data from over 200 signals or "clues" to try to guess what a human is looking for, then serve up results based on an engineered concept of what's important to human beings.

The Signals

Google regularly changes its algorithm to place emphasis on some signals over others, but here's a list of some of the most important factors the search giant considers when deciding which pages are relevant. This is by no means a comprehensive list, but it includes some of the most important:

On-Page Factors:

- Quality of the content

- How long people stay on a given page

- How "fresh" and substantial a web page's content is

- How ad-heavy a web page is

- How well HTML considerations like titles, descriptions, headers and structure describe and enhance the page

- How well the site architecture lends itself to search engine crawlers (spiders)

- How quickly the page loads

- How relevant URLs are to page topics

- How old your domain is, operating in the same way

- Mobile compatibility

Off-Page Factors:

- Do you have a Google+ Business page linked to your site

- Are you using rich snippets to display your picture on SERPs (Search Engine Result Pages)

- The quality of pages from which inbound links exist

- The relevance of outbound links

- The number of inbound links

- Whether you've purchased links

- Whether you've spammed other sites

- Whether you're a trusted authority

- Whether your site verifies its identity

- Whether your site hosts pirated content

- How often your content is shared on social media

- What country visitors are located in

- What city or local area visitors are located in

- Whether people regularly visit your site

- Whether your social media contacts have favored the site

The Evolution of the Algorithm

Google's search algorithm has undergone many drastic changes in the last fifteen years of doing business. In an effort to defeat spam artists and "dark arts" marketers, they regularly change their algorithm and signals to try and ensure that people using Google for search get the highest quality, most relevant pages. In 2013 is was estimated Google changed it's algorithm (or algo) an average of 2 times per day.

PageRank

This is one of the algorithms that Google uses to rank websites – and happens to also be the *first* algorithm they used back in 1998 when they launched. PageRank counts the number and quality of links to a given web page from other pages, which gives Google a sense of how "important" it is. PageRank is built on the assumption that important websites have many links from other sites.

Panda

Panda was a Google algorithm update in 2011 that attempted to lower the search rankings of low-quality sites and help Google's customers to find more relevant, high-quality sites. It was developed by human quality testers that visited thousands of sites and ranked them according to a list of factors of "What counts as a high-quality site," which Google then published online in an attempt to help webmasters "step into Google's mindset."

Penguin

Penguin was the name of Google's algorithm update back in spring of 2012 that attempted to decrease the rank of pages that were "gaming the system" using black-hat SEO techniques to deliberately manipulate the company's search index. According to Google, few websites actually lost their rankings for specific keywords, but those that did tended to be run by "dark arts" marketers that were filling their pages with thin, spammy content that didn't provide real value to web surfers.

Hummingbird

Google's newest algorithm change – code-named "Hummingbird" – was launched in September of 2013. It's the biggest change to the search engine's algorithm since 2010, when the company applied the "Caffeine Update," which was intended to optimize their indexing capability. Unlike Panda and Penguin, Hummingbird is not a tune-up, but an entirely new algorithm (even though it does use some parts of the old one.)

The point of Hummingbird was to make sure Google was equipped to handle modern search needs. As such, it's better equipped to handle concepts like "Conversational Search" and other, newer forms of accessing search engines. The algorithm is now more sensitive to the multiple possible meanings of individual words, rather than phrases.

What Else Did Hummingbird Change?

Another point of Hummingbird was to make a transition to "semantic search" – meaning search engine technology that works

harder to parse the meaning of customers'
search queries using smart engineering and a
healthy dose of artificial intelligence.

The artificial intelligence Google is
employing uses something called "inference
rules" to improve its search. Essentially, the
algorithm draws conclusions based on
premises and syntax in a user's search, and
then executes a formal logic procedure called
"forward chaining" to tease out what a
customer is actually searching for. It
accomplishes "chaining" by starting with the
data given by the customer and "reasoning"
(or a reasonable facsimile thereof) its way to a
hopefully accurate approximation of what
someone is looking for.

What Hummingbird Means

It means that search queries now get results
built around the holistic theme of the query,
rather than results that perfectly match certain
keywords. Once again, "content is king."
Google is solidly on the side of its users when
it comes to search rankings – folks that have a
problem or a question want high-quality
answers, not just a page filled with screaming,
blinking ads. Hummingbird was a powerful
move on Google's part to fight back against

unscrupulous marketers and spammers trying to use the search engine's popularity to sell products without offering people real value. It means that sites need to focus in on quality of their content.

It also means that you need to learn the new rules of Search Engine Optimization.

The Next Furry or Feathered Creature

Pandas and penguins and hummingbirds, oh my! So what is next for Google, now that the search giant has rolled out its latest incarnation? Recently, Google's Matt Cutts elucidated the company's "Moonshot changes" which included some important pieces of information that show the direction the company is headed in. One of the most revealing topics within "Moonshot" was a concept called Deep Learning.

Deep Learning

Google is focusing on something called "Deep Learning" that allows users – especially those searching by voice – to refine their searches within a pre-established context. For instance, if you were traveling, and wanted to know the weather in both your city of departure and arrival, you wouldn't have to search "what's the weather in x?" and "what's the weather in y?" You could ask "What's the weather in x?" and once you had the results, ask, "What about in y?" This is important, because it shows that Google has a strong focus on making search intuitive for people, and engineering their search engine around the natural, organic way that users communicate, rather than forcing them to adopt a new linguistic or technical modality in order to use their service.

Going Forward

Matt Cutts identified several trends at Google that can give you an idea of what the company is trying to accomplish in the coming years:

- The importance of mobile. The computing market is becoming increasingly dominated by smartphones, and more and more people use their phones to access the Web every day. Cutts stressed the importance of mobile optimization.

- Artificial intelligence. Hummingbird was just the beginning – Google is apparently working on training their systems to be able to read at an elementary school level so that it can better deliver search results to users.

- Spam-fighting through authorship. Google has begun making tools available for people to tie their identities to an authorship profile in order to fight spam, and has started identifying high-quality authors to feature more prominently in their results.

- Fighting ad-heavy websites. Some websites are lacking in aesthetics – or in some cases, are downright difficult to use – because of the preponderance of advertising on them. Google wants people finding high-quality content through their search engine, so they have already begun to take steps to combat this.

- Guest blogging as a way to gain links back to your site is out. As Mr. Cutts recently stated this used to be a "respectable" thing to do but has become spammy and should be avoided.

What Can I Do?

Simply put, you can work with Google to make sure your web page is as friendly to their crawlers and algorithms as possible. The process by which you accomplish that is called Search Engine Optimization. While true, relying solely on Google for guidance in this area is like asking your banker for the keys to the vault. It's probably not going to happen.

What is Search Engine Optimization?

Search Engine Optimization (also known as SEO) is all about optimizing your website to rank as highly as possible on search engines. It's sometimes known as "Organic Search," because it differs from Pay-Per-Click advertising in that you don't have to pay for each individual that sees your listing (pay per impression) or clicks (pay per click) on your link, but more on that later.

Why Do You Need to Do It?

SEO is highly effective and extremely low-cost over the long-term. With hundreds of millions of people using Google, having your site rank near the top of certain searches will give you a massive boost in the amount of people who visit your page. Once you've got a high ranking, that Web traffic just rolls in to your site on a daily basis, and you don't pay for a single impression or click.

However, it's important to keep in mind that SEO is a continuous process. It requires regular, consistent maintenance in order to keep your business listed as near to the top of the search results as possible. Your content must be relevant to popular searches, and you have to keep building links to lead search engine bots to your content.

On-Page Optimization

Now that Hummingbird is in full effect, here is what is working in On-Page SEO:

Meta Tags

Meta tags are little snippets of code that are located in the "head" of your web page. Behind the scenes, they give Google bots some of the necessary information about your web page that Google will use to determine its relevance to a search. There are four meta tags

to consider; here is how to best optimize
them:

- Title Tag – You see this in the top of
  the browser; it's viewed by search
  engines as the "title" of the page. This
  is the most important meta tag for
  SEO, and helps determine your page's
  relevance.

- Meta Keywords Attribute – these are
  the keywords you've decided are
  relevant to your page. They have very
  little impact on Google, but other
  search engines still use them in their
  algorithms. The most important
  function of this meta tag is in-site
  navigation; if people want to know
  more about a certain topic, they can
  click one of these tags and get a list of
  every article you've designated as
  relevant if you have enabled this in
  your WordPress setup.

- Meta Description Attribute – this is a
  short description of the page that
  shows up as a "snippet" below the title
  (as a summary) on a Search Engine
  Results Page. This is important
  because it's essentially your teaser or

advertisement to get people to click on your link.

- Meta Robots Attribute – this is an indication to Google's bots of what they should do with the page when they encounter it. There are two yes or no questions: Should the bot index the page, or not? And should the bot follow links on your pages, or not? In most cases, the answers are yes and yes.

Keywords

Once you've created the content you want to share with your audience, you need to identify the keywords and phrases on search engines that you're targeting. Google Analytics mostly no longer provides this information, so you'll have to get crafty and creative in targeting keywords you think people are searching for. However there are alternatives, Google "google analytics alternatives".

You also need to check how competitive your targeted keywords are. If you're trying to buy up phrases related to "home remodel," for instance, you're going to be competing with thousands – if not hundreds of thousands – of other sites also jockeying for traffic. As a general rule, you want to be more specific when determining what search terms to incorporate into your content.

Once you've got your specific keywords or phrases, you want to naturally incorporate them into your copy. The bots no longer measure keyword density – that is, how many times a search phrase comes up on a web page – so don't just "stuff" your articles with keywords in order to get a higher ranking. That was a regular tactic in SEO pre-Hummingbird, and it resulted in jilted, terrible copy that can be near unreadable to most people. If you do this now, Google will determine that your site's quality is low, thus hurting your rank on the search results page.

Keyword Variations and Latent Semantic Indexing (LSI)

Essentially, a keyword variation is a simple differentiation of a root keyword. People's phrasing can vary dramatically even if they're searching for the same thing. For this reason, it's important to target variations of keywords. You need to see the bigger picture of what people are looking for online. Someone searching for "guitar lessons" is, plain and simple, hoping to find guitar lessons. But they may search in many different ways for that. So if your root keyword phrase is "guitar lessons," you'll want to target keyword phrases like "how to play guitar," "lessons for guitar," "guitar teacher," etc.

Typically, you would want to figure out ways to slip these phrases into the content of your web page, by phrasing and rephrasing. However, if you find that variations of your root keyword phrase are significantly different from the topic of your blog post or page, it only helps your site to add more pages focusing on the varied phrases.

Since Hummingbird, one of the most important things you need to know about target keywords is that long-tail keywords perform better than short ones. You want your phrases to be longer than three words whenever possible. This helps Google understand the intent of your page better, and though they tend to have lower search volume, they also have lower competition levels, which means you can rank better within your market niche or market vertical.

The key now is to write your content first, incorporating your keyword phrase once, and then to restate it in different ways throughout the rest of the copy (using keyword variations.) This is taking advantage of Hummingbird's Latent Semantic Indexing (LSI) feature. Paul Dean over at Wealthy Affiliate has a great example of LSI-optimized copy. Here's his example paragraph, with the LSI words highlighted:

"Visit Thrashadog for all your **dog training** requirements. Here we take **our job** seriously, and provide and **teach** all forms of **canine correction**, tailored to your pet's disposition. If you'd like to **have your dog taught** to **walk to heel, sit at a kerb, avoid other dogs**, or just be **better behaved**, then give us a call and we'll introduce you both to the finest **training** in the South West!"

Google now uses AI (Artificial Intelligence) to understand that many of these terms are related to the same theme - in Paul Dean's example, it's obviously dog training. Notice that it picks up words like "teach, canine correction, taught, avoid other dogs, better behaved" and others that are contextually related to the keyword search.

What does that mean?   It means that your copy needs to be readable and compelling, or you'll get hit with a double whammy: Google will figure out that you're trying to game the old system and lower your rank, and potential customers won't stick around long enough for you to convert them anyway.

Off-Page Optimization

Raising your search ranking isn't wholly dependent on what's *on* your site. It also has to do with activities that are outside its borders. Remember that Google is always looking for indicators of what makes website quality, and one of the best indicators it's got is how the world perceives your page. So a website that gets referenced a lot (by other pages linking to it) and is mentioned on social media (such as Facebook, Twitter, Pinterest and so on) is considered higher quality. So what can you do besides site design and construction that will help raise your rank?

Link Building

While social media is an incredibly important part of off-page optimization, it has its own chapter in this book, so here we're going to focus on the non-social media process of link building in the post-Hummingbird era.

For a long time, links were the centerpiece of the Google search algorithm. The more pages that linked to a given page, the more authoritative it became. Then, dark-arts marketers (translated: spammers) came along and started gaming the system, and Google had to start being more selective – although they still base their algorithm in a large part around inbound links! These days, it's not about the *number* of inbound links your page gets, but the *quality*, as well. Getting a link from a random Tumblr blog doesn't get you the same heft as a link from a writer for *The Wall Street Journal*, for instance.

No one from the *Journal* is going to link to your page when you first launch it, so you'll have to start small. But it's better to think of link building as link earning. In order to build inbound links to your page, you've got to give people a reason to do so – to "earn" their link. Usually, this is done by publishing high-quality content, such as blog posts, how-to articles, videos and more. The art of creating content is its own beast, and also has its own chapter in this book, so file that away for a bit.

Post-Hummingbird Link Building

For a long time, marketers built links to their page using keyword analysis to figure out which terms they should build links for. It was all about anchor text (the text the link is "behind") and precise keyword targeting, and marketers could simply find a few keywords, buy a few links or blog posts that had their designated anchor text, and get a good ranking.

No longer. Post-Hummingbird, keywords are still important, but they've changed. Exact match domains, anchor text and most paid links can still be effective but are a lot less effective than they used to be, and will only get less effective as search engines get better (and "smarter") through their use of artificial intelligence.

Now that Google is trying to figure out what a user is searching for without explicit context with LSI, link building has to be reorganized around keyword synonyms, the theme of sites you want a link from, the credibility of pages that are linking to you, and more. Link building is no longer an SEO tactic – it's a holistic *strategy* for outreach and content creation.

Notice a pattern here? Google is trying to get away from SEO as a way for marketers to make a quick buck, and trying to make webmasters focus on *quality* first. So when you're looking to build links, it's not enough to go out and just create some other pages that link to each other in order to get a good rating. You've got to build relationships with other pages, provide quality content and reach out to authorities and opinion makers within your industry to build natural, organic digital networks. Essentially, if you want to convince people that your site is worth coming to, *your site has to be worth coming to* – and you've got to prove it.

Alternatives: Pay-Per-Click (PPC) Advertising

Unless you've been living in a digital cave for the last couple of decades (give or take) you're already familiar with pay-per-click advertising. Essentially, it's an ad model whereby an advertiser runs an ad on a website and pays the webmaster whenever the ad gets displayed or clicked.

In this chapter, you'll get a comprehensive introduction to pay-per-click advertising so that you can understand how to use paid search to generate more leads and close more sales. As with the rest of the book, the most important platform you need to learn is Google, so this chapter will deal entirely with Google's paid search program, which is called Google AdWords. Once you know how AdWords works, you've got a solid foundation on which to build knowledge about other search engines, since they're all basically following in Google's footsteps. However please note PPC on social media sites such as Facebook should be approached somewhat differently since the audience on social media sites is different from those doing Google searches.

Paid and Organic Search

Marketing through a search engine is one of the primary forms in Internet marketing, and it comes in two varieties: Paid and Organic. Organic search comes from SEO, which we discussed in the previous chapter. Paid search lets you pay Google to display a link to your site on the search engine results page (SERP) whenever someone types in particular keywords or phrases. The SERP displays the ads (created by you) and you pay Google for the amount of people that either see or click your ad based on how you set up your ads payment options.

According to Mike Moran at Business 2 Community, about one quarter of all search clicks are on paid search ads, with the remainder skipping straight to organic results. 25% doesn't sound like a lot – so why even bother with paid links? Because paid links are a terrific option if you're not ranking high with organic search. And remember there are "billions" of searches per day.

Paid Search Is Not A Replacement

There are a lot of ways to use paid search – including some ways you definitely *should,* as opposed to those you definitely *should not.* The first thing you need to know as a small business is that paid search is not a replacement for the old phonebook or classified ads you ran in the pre-Internet days. Just being on a search engine doesn't bring you traffic. Likewise, just because you're doing paid search doesn't mean you can ignore SEO. Essentially, the lesson here is that paid search doesn't replace any other efforts – it adds to them.

It's best to think of paid search as a complement to your other marketing efforts – a way to optimize your coverage of the search engines. Your SEO efforts should be working hard to get you to the top of your critical keyword searches, and your paid search should help you "cover" the ground that SEO isn't making up. Remember that while blogging, driving leads and SEO may be the main thrust of your focus, the more information that you can get from your inbound marketing campaigns, the more you can apply that intelligence to an effective paid search campaign.

Paid search will also assist you in presenting credibility to your potential customers. The more coverage you've got on the search engine results page, the more authoritative you appear, which not only helps users make the decision to click your link, but also (over time) may attract good links from around the Web, which will continue to amplify your SEO efforts.

What You Are Capable of With Paid Search

Beyond the initial, overarching goal of driving traffic to your site, there are other useful things you can accomplish with paid search.

- A/B testing. Paid search is one of the most important tools you've got for testing, optimizing and iterating your landing pages through a process called A/B testing, a very important part of Internet marketing. Here's how it works for ads: You can have multiple ads on a single keyword or keywords. Google will rotate the display of the ads and track which ads get the most clicks. Then you can easily see which ads attract more clicks and therefore which are more effective and use those. Here's how it works for landing pages (the pages your ad clicks go to): You can run one ad on Google, but customize it so that it goes to two different landing pages (for instance, it may send every other user to one of these given web pages.) You can use these two different landing pages to test features, offers, layouts, pictures – whatever it takes to figure out what is bringing in the most traffic and converting the highest number of leads.

- Keyword research. Paid search can help you find new keywords and keyword phrases to use in your marketing campaigns. Google AdWords will generate a report called Search Terms that lets you know which keywords your ad has been displayed for – it's not always the exact match you paid for, but it's usually semantically linked. For instance, if you bid on the keyword phrase "blue car," Google might show your ad when a user searches for "blue sports car" even though you didn't bid on that exact phrase, because that's what the user was looking for. In this case, on the left column of the report there will be a little green box that says "Added" next to keywords that you aren't currently bidding on. This is essentially a list of what people are actually searching for — so it's valuable information for you to put to work. This report will also let you know the conversion rate of certain keywords, so you know which phrases to focus in on (and which to use for SEO.)

- Enhancing SEO campaigns. Even if you're the top SEO guru around and you've got your site ranking #1 on certain searches, you don't want to exclude paid search from your strategy. Yes, Google is working hard to use LSI and other artificial intelligence methods to increase its semantic understanding of people's searches. But different sites are going to rank higher on different search terms — even if they're semantically similar — because of SEO. If you're the top page for one or two search terms, you may want to do your research and figure out where you're not – then run paid advertisements in those spaces so your brand is popping up across the spectrum of what folks are searching for.

Crafting Your Paid Search Campaign

Paid search campaigns are made up of three basic components: Keywords, advertisements and landing pages. The first step is selecting the keywords you'll give to Google. Google will then show your ads on its results page to anyone searching for those keywords. The ads need to be designed for these keyword searches – that is, the text of them needs to be both alluring to customers and relevant to search terms – in order to get folks to your landing page. Lastly, the job of your landing page is to get people to convert in one way or another – by either making a purchase, signing up for a service/newsletter, downloading something, etc. Any paid search campaign needs to manage these three components.

Pay-Per-Click

Pay-per-click is a part of paid search. It means that you don't pay to display your ad; you only pay when someone clicks on it. There are other forms of paid search, such as CPM (called pay-per-impression advertising) that may give ads more display time. If you are expecting a large number of clicks CPM may be more cost effective since you are not paying for clicks but rather impressions or when an ad shows on a page. Unfortunately sometimes the only way to determine which is best, PPC or CPM, is by measuring the results and costs of each.

The amount you pay per click depends on how well you do in Google's "auction." You have to bid on a keyword, and your bid determines your placement (if any) on Google's SERP. It's important to understand that your bid is not necessarily what you'll pay per click on your ad. In fact, the lowest bid on a keyword or keyword phrase will set the "base" price of the "lowest" ad placement on the page, and then the prices for the other placements will be priced incrementally higher according to the value of their "real estate" on the page (in general, higher on the page is almost always better.)

Quality Score

But wait – your bid isn't the only factor in whether or not Google serves up your ad in conjunction with certain keywords and keyword phrases. There is also an algorithm Google uses called "Quality Score" that attempts to assess the relevancy of both your ad and your landing page to the search term. This is so that unscrupulous marketers can't buy up keywords that direct people to completely irrelevant pages, and so that Google users get a better search experience overall.

Quality Score is a scale of 1 to 10 (1 being lowest, 10 being highest.) displayed for each ad. A competitor of yours might be willing to bid *higher* on a search term, but if their ad isn't as relevant as yours, you might still end up with the top spot on the SERP. This is a huge benefit to small, local businesses, who may not have the advertising budget to go after big, broad keyword phrases, but who can laser-target hyper-local search terms (think "home improvement store in x neighborhood) without worrying about being outbid by some corporation with deep pockets and a penchant for squashing little guys.

Quality Score is also an important tool for researching keywords. If you bid on a keyword and find that Google gives you a low Quality Score, that's a good indication that your site is not well-optimized for that particular keyword, so it's probably not a cost-efficient channel for you. By looking for the right keywords and keyword phrases that return high Quality Scores to you, you can get the most out of your paid search budget.

Keyword Match Types

There are a mind-boggling amount of variations and combinations of ways people can input search terms into Google. Thus, Google offers five keyword match types you can use to specify when and how to display your ads. They are:

1. Exact match. If you set a keyword to "exact match," your ad will only display when people type in your exact keyword phrase in the exact order you specify. In order to do this, you'll surround your keywords in brackets. For example: [keyword phrase]. This

is valuable when you're trying to nail down a highly specific search audience. The flipside of this, of course, is that you've got a highly specific search audience – meaning you've got drastic limits on who you're reaching. After all, there's no way to tell the exact way that people will search for what they're looking for, so even if you bid on a long list of potential exact matches, you're missing out on a lot of leads and customers who are using other combinations of keyword phrases and search terms.

2. Phrase match. In this case, your ad will display if people type in the same order of words, but also include other words. For instance, if you bought the phrase "keyword phrase" and someone typed in "new keyword phrase" your ad would still pop up. As in the previous example, surround your keyword in quotation marks to make them phrase match.

3. Broad match. In order to refine your strategy, you can set your ads to display whenever the search term contains a

combination of the words in your keyword phrase without regard for order. To do this, just don't surround your keyword with anything. You may think this is the best way to do all of your advertising, since it gets the most possible traffic. However, remember that it's not all about quantity, it's also about quality. If there are a lot of people searching for something that happens to include your search term, but isn't terribly relevant to their search, you'll get a lot of traffic but not a lot of qualified leads. Unless you're trying to raise brand awareness on a large scale, high traffic does not translate into high dollar amounts.

4. Modified Broad match or Extended Broad match. Is basically a more specific broad match. For example by placing a "+" sign, called a broad match modifier, in front of any word in a keyword phrase forces the search to return only results that have that word or close variations like singulars or plurals in them. This can be helpful to keep your add from displaying on unrelated SERPs a broad match returns

but keeps your match broader than exact or phrase matches.

5. Negative match. If you want your ads to pop up for certain searches within a given potential set but not others, negative match is the way to go. Let's say you wanted to advertise that you sold used cars, and wanted to refine your advertising to make sure you were reaching folks in the market for a used, not a new car. In this case, you wouldn't want your ads to show to folks who are searching for new cars, so you'd want Google to ignore all searches containing the word "new" when displaying your ads. To do this, designate keywords with a minus sign. For example: -new.

Crafting a Keyword Strategy

With all of the possible options, what's the best course of action for your business to take? The only answer is the one you don't want to hear: *It depends on your business and your strategy*. But in general, you'll find that using a combination of the 5 match types will help you drive traffic. Then close examination of your Search Terms reports will help you find the keywords and ad combinations that are converting well and make sense for your business and strategies. Once you've got that information, you can start setting some keyword phrases to exact match, because you've got the data proving that they'll do the trick.

In essence, crafting a keyword strategy is like crafting any component of your marketing efforts – experiment, measure, modify, repeat. Later in this book, you'll find a chapter on performance metrics you can use to help you refine and optimize your strategy. The important thing is that you never think you've found "what works" because "what works" is going to continually shift and evolve over time, and your strategy needs to do the same.

Structuring Your Account

Google AdWords has you set up your account in a certain structure – and the way in which you do can make or break the success of your paid search efforts. First, you've got your keywords, and the list of keywords you're going to bid on. Then, you've got the ads you're going to have Google display when someone uses a search term including one of the keywords. This list of keywords is called an "ad group." You put related keywords in an ad group, and write copy for the ads that's as relevant as possible and the most likely to get someone to click on it.

If you have several different products or services you want to advertise, you can also organize your ad groups by "campaign." This allows you to have different, highly targeted ads for different campaigns.

The Daily Budget Cap

This can be the most important component of any AdWords campaign so please pay very close attention. Google doesn't charge you individually for each click. Rather, you give them a daily limit on how much you're willing to spend per campaign. This way you can tailor how often your ads get seen without breaking the bank. If, however, you find yourself coming upon a rash of crazy days where you have several click-heavy hours in the morning, thus depleting your daily budget, you can also ask Google to spread your ads throughout the day.

The daily budget cap is useful for small businesses, because you can start with a low budget and immediately begin tinkering with different keyword/copy combinations that will optimize your ads' success. Once you've found a combination that works, you'll be able to increase your spending on par with your rising click through rate and lead quality.

One thing to note: Google will attempt to spend your budget every day, but if you've got a rarefied keyword phrase that not many folks are searching for, the company just might not be able to get you out in front of people's eyes. If you find that Google can't place your ad with enough frequency, it's time to go back and review your keyword strategy to ensure you're targeting the right subset of searchers.

Alternatives: Content Marketing

The Web is all about content, so this age-old marketing strategy has enjoyed a dramatic resurgence in recent years.

What Is Content Marketing?

Content marketing is the act of creating *valuable* and *relevant* content for your target audience, with three goals in mind:

1. Establishing and strengthening your brand.

2. Building trust in your authority.

3. Driving sales.

Essentially, you provide high-quality content for people to consume, and in return, they get to know, like, and trust you. That content could be anything from blog posts to how-to articles to books to e-books to videos. The key is that the content provides value to the consumer, and is presented and available free of charge. As consumers come to trust and appreciate the content, their feelings will transfer over into a perception of your company as an authority (which is a valuable thing on today's noisy Web), as well as conferring brand loyalty and higher sales on your business.

Getting Started With Content Marketing

If you have decided that Content Marketing is the right approach for your business, you'll need to get started with a comprehensive strategy. The first step is defining your audience – what drives them? What interest them? What brings them together? The next step is creating content that will be meaningful to them.

In a sense, you have an advantage as a small business when it comes to content marketing. Because you're smaller, you can focus tightly on a single niche and become a trusted authority – also, consumers within niche markets tend to have to overcome larger barriers of trust with large corporations. Consumers can buy into the idea that a small business owner wants to be a normal, functioning member of their niche community. They automatically (and probably rightfully) suspect the motivations of a large, corporate interest.

But how do you create quality, meaningful content? That's an art and a science, and merits its own book, but the pillar is remembering the 5 W's: Who, What, Where,

When and Why (and don't forget How, when necessary!)

Who Are You Making Content For?

Who is your following? Are you sure you know who is really interested in the product you're trying to sell? If you don't, how can you create content they'll find relevant, valuable and useful? It's crucial to understand as much as possible about your customers so that you can provide them solutions – first in the form of content, and soon in the form of your product or service.

What Content Are You Delivering?

For most folks, the term "content marketing" immediately conjures the image of a blog post. But that's not the way some folks prefer to consume content – they prefer videos, InfoGraphics, podcasts, images, memes, whitepapers – you name it. The more diverse and unique the media with which you make content available, the more people will find your content approachable.

When Are Your Customers Consuming Content?

If you're like most businesses, you'll notice that you get more interaction with your content around 9 AM and 5 PM in your own time zone. But what if you develop followers around the country? Or around the world? You'll need to experiment with the right times to publish or share content in order to maximize the amount of people who have access to it.

Where Are Your Customers At?

Where are your customers going? If they're relatively young, you'll want to look for them on Instagram. If they're primarily female, you'll want to find them on Pinterest. You can find just about anyone on Facebook or YouTube – and now you're starting to get the point. Marketing 101 is "go to where the audience is." You've got to find out where they're at, and distribute your content on the platforms they're already using.

Why Are You Creating Content?

That is, what are you trying to accomplish? If you're only content marketing "to make money for your business" people are going to realize that, and they won't want to consume and engage with your content. You've got to remember that the reason you're content marketing is to connect with people in an authentic way and build their perception of you as an authority. In order to do that, you've got to know what your customers are really interested in and build on that.

Also, are you sure your content is even any good? If you're not a naturally skilled writer, you might want to look into hiring a professional to freelance some posts for you. Ditto with any of your other content. If you don't publish quality, tangible content, you're reinforcing your voice and your brand – but in a bad way. Your content should communicate exactly in the way you want consumers to receive your business – so be sure to constantly evaluate the tone, message and quality of your content to ensure people not only derive significant value from it, but are interpreting it in the correct way.

The Importance Of Research

It's a dreaded word: Research. It's never anywhere near as much fun as writing a great blog post or making a content-rich video, but it's critical to the success of your content marketing efforts and the #1 most important task identified by professional copywriters.

The point of research is to build a profile of your *ideal customer*. What does he or she look like? What are his or her demographics information and consumption behaviors? What are his or her problems and pain points that you intend to solve with your product or service? Once you know what your ideal customer looks like, you can start building content that speaks directly to him or her.

Here is the step-by-step process for researching and building the profile of that ideal customer:

1. Get out in the world. You didn't just start a business to make money – you started a business because you're passionate about your work, a buyer in your own industry, and a member of the community that uses your products or services. To effectively reach your

market, you've got to get out among them and figure out what they're talking about. This means connecting with people on social media, other blogs, community forums and chat boards to figure out what people need – and don't need – from a small business in your industry. Once you've identified your customers, you can start putting out content that is relevant and valuable to them. Of course, if you're out there participating in relevant forums and social media platforms, remember that the key word is "participating," not "spamming." People don't mind advertisements and marketing – but they immediately label it as spam if it comes from outside their community, or it feels like someone is trying to take advantage of them. You need to contribute to conversations, take notes on things that people say that's interesting, figure out folks' pet peeves, what they think is cool and passé, and what their values are.

2. Find the right keywords. The days of Google feeding marketers data on keywords is over. Now, it's all about

footwork and research to figure out what people are searching for. This can be confusing, especially when trying to separate the signal from the noise. But it's crucially important! You need to be able to optimize your web page for search engines, and you also need keyword data to help you set yourself apart in the market and get ahead of your competitors. Savvy keyword research will let you create content that solves your customers' problems before any of your competitors can. If you're offering quality, valuable content where others are throwing up useless, nonspecific information on the same topics, you'll establish yourself as a trusted authority in no time.

3. Know your competition. You need to know more about your market than just what kind of customers are out there – you have to know about your competitors, too. What do they excel at where you fall behind? Where are you crushing them? In the same way you build a profile of your ideal customer, you have to also build a

profile of your competitors. What kinds of products or services do they offer? What kind of content are they sharing on their blog or website? Are they marketing on social media? Are they any good at it? How is their SEO – and their ranking in the search engines results pages? What are their content marketing strengths and weaknesses? Also, remember that you need to find out more than just the big competitors – markets are never disrupted by large corporations. It's always up-and-coming small businesses just like yours that enter a market and upend everything. So be aware of which companies are launching what kind of content, and which bloggers in your sphere are starting to attract attention so you don't get blindsided by a major market disruption.

4. Be consistent. Olympic athletes don't get to their level without constant practice, and you won't become a world-class researcher without doing it on a regular basis, either. At first, you'll be a little clumsy in your research, but the only way to get better is to do it,

measure it, tweak it and iterate – on and on to infinity. If you're not constantly researching, moving and constantly changing, you're dead in the water.

What Great Copy Looks Like

Far and away, the most common form of Web content is copy. Whether it's blog posts, white papers, InfoGraphics, how-to articles…you name it. Copy is what drives the Internet.

Copy has a bad name for good reasons. Most of it is absolutely awful tripe that barely manages to communicate without making a consumers' eyes glaze over. It's so much fluff without substance – all sizzle and no steak, if you like. Copy should work like a magic show – it should keep people focused on the "wow" factor while allowing the magician (okay, the writer) to keep the amazing stuff coming. Think about it – if you go to a magic show, a lot of people have paid for tickets to sit down and be fooled on purpose. They know it's not real, but they want to be amazed. Copy should also be magical – it's there to serve a purpose, which is to increase your sales and establish you as a trusted authority, but it has to do so in a way that doesn't insult the audience's intelligence and keeps them hooked for more.

Here are the three elements of magical copy:

1. The headline compels you to read the first sentence. When someone lands on your page, you've got a few seconds to capture their attention. That means your words have to act decisively and powerfully. The headline is one of the most crucial elements of content marketing.

2. It's long past time that copywriters started taking a lesson from great fiction authors. Consider some of the great opening sentences of the greatest novels ever written. They are simple, but convey a promise of complexity. They are (usually) short, but take up a lot of metaphysical space. They happen in the present, but reach back into the past and extend into the future. Now, imagine crafting a headline that managed to convey the physical characteristics of your content, what it

looks like, the demographic it's aimed at, the intangible qualities, and which also manages to convey something about the intangible qualities. Will anyone fail to move on to the first sentence?

3. So let's take a very blasé headline, pulled from this article, which comes up on the first page of Google when you search for content marketing: "What is Content Marketing? – The Content Marketing Institute." Well. It seems to match a keyword well, which is good for SEO purposes. And we know who wrote it – it's apparently some sort of authority on content marketing, because they're an institute. But now consider this headline: "Write Content, Write Now: 5 Essential How-To Principles from the Content Marketing Institute." Look how much more this sentence is doing. There's a pun in the headline that causes someone to take a second look (a double-take is great for getting past the attention threshold with web surfers.) It's using a number, which sets reader expectations up front and gives them

an idea of the length and scope of the piece. It tells people what the piece will be – a how-to, not some random article that looks like someone just took the Wikipedia entry and replaced a few of the words with synonyms. It uses a powerful adjective and noun combination – these are principles, not "tips" or "tricks" and they are essential, not "weird" or "strange." To top it all off, these "essential principles" are from a place called the Content Marketing Institute – this is an institute specifically formed for Content Marketing, not some schmo freelance "writer" who got hired to regurgitate someone else's copy in a slightly different form for $2/hour.

4. See the difference? The only problem with this headline is that it may not conform to the best SEO keyword phrases out there. No problem. Write the headline first, then incorporate the keyword phrase afterward. Not the other way around. Ever. That will just get you boring, awful headlines.

5. Writing a great headline is not easy to do, but mimicking a great headline is.

Start paying attention as you surf around the web and start looking for formats that incorporate these guidelines. It's okay to replicate a sentence structure in your headline, so be shameless and write down the best, most compelling headlines you come across, then do your best impression of them when you're writing your own headlines. Remember that the headline has to do a lot of work in order to get someone to read that first sentence, so if you put the time and effort you need into a proper headline, you'll ensure people get there. And once you've gotten people to the first sentence, you're ready for the second element of magical copy...

6. The first sentence compels you to read the second sentence. And the second sentence compels you to read the third, and so on. Ever watched a great television show like Downton Abbey or Game of Thrones? Even when things are slow and an episode is nothing but an hour's worth of dialogue, you can't rip your eyes away. The narrative has done such a good job

of hooking you with every single line
that not only do you keep watching,
you get heartburn just thinking you'll
have to wait another week to see a new
episode. This is because each scene
does one of three things: It makes a
promise to viewers, raises the stakes on
an earlier promise, or simultaneously
delivers on a promise while making a
new one. That's it. There's never a
time where the audience isn't hanging
on the edge, waiting for the fulfillment
of an earlier promise. This is how great
copy should read, as well. There's an
amazing post I can't recommend highly
enough to people called "How to
Manipulate Your Audience Like
Downton Abbey." Forget the negative
connotations associated with the word
"manipulate." That's exactly what a
good writer does, but we do it for a
willing audience (remember the
magician example from before?)

7. The sentences and words are highly
   readable. Most newspapers are written
   at between a fifth and eighth-grade
   reading level. Read that again – the
   New York Times writes articles that are

plain and simple enough that a preteen can read and understand it. If you're curious, this book is written at about a ninth grade reading level for the same reasons. It's not because it's aimed at ninth graders, it's because if you make people work too hard to read something, they won't finish it. No one likes to feel stupid. If you never read an entire Wikipedia article in your entire life, read this one on readability (you can also enjoy the irony late in the article when it becomes highly difficult to read.) When you're considering the readability of your copy, at its most basic level, you need to pay attention to these three things:

a) How many words per sentence? In general, the less words you have per sentence, the better. When you're writing copy, it's never okay to use a semicolon; since the point of that is to join two independent clauses, you should just make them a separate sentence. (Yes, that last semicolon was on purpose.)

b) What's the average grade level of words? Never forget that you're writing web copy. Although there is something incredible and artistic and beautiful about discovering the perfect word for the perfect context, that needs to be kept to artistic literature, not the craft of copy, because you're not creating art. You're crafting copy in an artistic way. Contriving chichi prose as some sort of verbose odium to present your perspicacity is just garish and obdurate. See? It makes you look like a poser.

c) How long are the words? English is a funny language – we have many, many synonyms for closely related words, unlike many other languages that rely on context to shade what we mean (except that English will also use context to shade meaning.) It's one of the most difficult languages to learn on the planet – perhaps the most difficult – because there are so many words that have such different meanings and so many random rules. Generally, English words have at least one short version of a word and at least one long version (though not in all cases. Again, with the haphazardness of English.) The short version is usually Germanic and used in everyday speech, and the long version is usually Latinate and better suited for very specific linguistic situations, like certain kinds of writing. Consider the words "love" and "adoration." They mean slightly different things, but they're synonyms. However, "love" is short and Germanic and "adoration" is long and Latinate. Whenever possible, go with short and Germanic. The better people's eyes can flow across the page, the better off you will be.

Crafting A Content Marketing Strategy

Crafting a winning content marketing strategy takes a light and deft touch. You need a wide assortment of different tactics just to effectively reach one niche, much less the entire population. But by developing a strong content marketing strategy, you can guide your approach in a sustainable way that gives your target audience the individual experiences they demand, that are appropriate to each niche you're trying to work your way in to, and that will ensure your content is seen and shared by a wide variety of people.

Now, if you're interested in blowing through your precious marketing resources as quickly as possible without getting absolutely any gain, the best way to do it is through scattershot, gut-check marketing tactics. You know – trying a whole bunch of different things that "feel right" without unifying your tactics under goal-oriented strategies.

When you're developing a content marketing strategy, use a simple acronym called PLACE:

1. **Planning.** Every good strategy begins with planning. First thing first: You'll

need to establish your vision and mission – that is, what do you want your strategy to do? It's the same as when you wrote your business plan. You need to set goals and steps to achieve those goals at the onset. You also need to plan how you're going to create and leverage compelling online content to accomplish all of these goals. You don't need to create all of the content yourself, and you shouldn't try! There are a lot of really good marketers out there making amazing stuff, and it costs you nothing to share that content and reap the rewards. However, don't think you can just pass around trite copy, pictures borrowed from the first page of Google Images, or useless how-to-boil-water articles. Forget what you've heard: Marketing might be a numbers game, but in this post-Hummingbird world, *content marketing is not*. It is a *quality* game.

2. **Locating.** You know your target audience and their appropriate demographic. You've got the content that will appeal to them. Now, go out and find them! They're out there, just a

couple of clicks away. Use search engines, blogs and social networks to find the place your audience is already congregating online. Once you know where they are, you can join the discussions already in progress and begin to participate in the community. Once you're trusted, and not just a spammer, you can start disseminating links to your published content. Whenever possible, make sure that content allows the greatest possible leeway for consumers to take it and change it, run with it, take it to other platforms and, in as many ways as possible, interact with it. Images and memes are a great example of this. While you're in the locating phase, your important metrics are "friends" or "followers" on social media, visitors to your page and inbound links.

3. **Acting.** You've got your target audience and they're in their sphere. Now, it's all about keeping them there. Your content hub needs to stay packed to the brim with engaging, relevant, useful material. This means updating consistently, and keeping up a steady

stream of fresh stuff. Content is how you get permission from consumers to market to them and sell to them – by consistently providing them with content they'll return to again and again on your blog, website or online community, you'll earn that. Consider any successful newspaper or blog, how attractive would they be without engaging, relevant, useful content. The important metrics here are the amount of time people spend at your hub and how many leads you're generating.

4. **Converting.** This is where you take all that customer goodwill, generated by providing them with useful and interesting content, and convert it into sweet, sweet sales. Make sure you're focusing in on re-marketing, Email automation, data collection about the personal likes and dislikes of customers and honing in on as many repeat sales as you can manage. Your important metrics at this stage of the strategy are your revenue, the average value of an order, and of course, how many orders you're getting (or how many are telling

you they've come into your shop because of your web page.)

5. **Engaging.** This is a step in the process that's absolutely crucial, but so many businesses fail to get it right. If your customer isn't uniquely thrilled by your product or services, you've failed to get them not only as a repeat sale, but most importantly, as an ally sharing their testimony on social media and through word of mouth. A lot of marketers see an incomplete cycle – they think that as soon as you've got the customer pulling out their cash, they've done their job. But marketing extends long after the point of sale – and a small business owner who doesn't understand that is a small business owner who won't stay in business very long. Your key metrics here are repeat purchases and new referrals from satisfied customers.

Alternatives: Mobile Marketing

.Buoyed by ever more powerful technology, smartphones, tablets and other mobile computing devices have seen a meteoric rise to prominence, and now account for a substantial portion of people conducting Internet searches.

No Internet marketing strategy would be complete without reaching out to the mobile web. There are almost four billion mobile phones in the world – which is about four times more than there are desktop computers. You can't afford to miss out on marketing to hundreds of millions of people – many of whom are increasingly turning away from desktop computers entirely.

The Mobile Web

What is the mobile web? Well, you already know all about the "desktop" web – those are sites and pages constructed for people who are surfing from a PC or a Mac.

But if you've ever tried to visit a "desktop" website that hasn't been optimized for mobile, you know it can be difficult – tiny text, graphics that don't format properly, plug-ins that don't work. For this reason, millions of websites have designed special sites that don't require a large screen, a mouse and keyboard to use. These are called "mobile-optimized" sites, and that's what we mean when we say "the mobile web."

There are two main areas where the mobile web shines. The first is utility: Smartphones with mobile web functionality allow people to check-in at the airport, transfer funds in their bank accounts and perform other tasks that would have taken much more time and effort in years past. The other is, of course, entertainment. Whether you're riding the subway, waiting in a lobby or just want to kill some time, the mobile Web is great for reading a little gossip about Hollywood stars or firing up a quick game and launching some enraged avians at green pigs (think the Angry Birds game).

Designing a Mobile Website

Of course, anything that goes on your desktop site should go on your mobile site – essentials like contact information, directions or a map, and an "about" page so that folks can learn about your business. The difference is that your site needs to be optimized for devices with small screens, limited keyboards and touchscreens. Here are five essentials for any mobile site:

1. *Remember that mobile users surf differently than desktop users.* When folks are surfing on their phones, they are usually not hunting for long reads, and their connection tends to be slower, so they want quick access to short amounts of content. <u>Check out this post from Vocus.com on 50 mobile search statistics.</u> <u>Including that 70% of searches will result in a sale in the near future from Televox.com.</u>

2. *Keep it simple and elegant.* When writing copy for your mobile site, use direct sentences, and keep them short! Be sure that navigation is as easy as possible (with as few clicks or touches as possible) and remember that folks don't want to take the time to fill out long forms on their phones, because it's less wieldy to do so with their smaller keyboards.

3. *Make sure the site loads as quickly as possible.* This is a truism just about anywhere,

desktop or mobile, but it's especially crucial for mobile because many folks access the Internet over 3G or 4G connections, which tend to be substantially slower than Wi-Fi or Ethernet. Videos, animations and large images can slow down your page's load times, so keep them as minimal as possible.

4. *Make sure the site is useful.* You're not designing a mobile site for your business, you're designing the site for your audience. That cannot be stressed too much. Make sure you're providing what they need, especially when they're on the go.

5. *Make sure the site works across all phones and platforms.* It doesn't do to have a layout that looks great on an iPhone but terrible on a Galaxy Tab. There is a wide array of diverse mobile devices, and a site that looks fantastic on one might not even work on another. You've got to rigorously test your phone on as many platforms as possible (iPhone, Android, Windows Phone) and on as many phones within platforms as possible to be sure you're not

accidentally frustrating your potential customers. If not you then someone else, but it must be done.

Text Message (SMS) Marketing

Of course, the Web isn't all smartphones can do. Most of us also use text messaging on a regular basis – and it's proving fertile ground for small businesses who incorporate it into their marketing strategy. Text messaging is also advantageous because there is still a large portion of the population without a smartphone, but their older model cell phones can still receive Short Message Service – also known as SMS.

Naturally, SMS marketing isn't for every business, but it's a solid way to communicate with customers about any promotions, contests, discounts or other campaigns you're running that you think would appeal to a younger, mobile-wielding crowd.

SMS marketing is effective when it's consistently employed – meaning that you should communicate with your mobile customers at least every 90 days so they aren't surprised when they get a text message from you. But somewhat paradoxically, SMS marketing isn't effective for long-term promotions. Since people usually have a certain amount of texts they can send or receive per month (and some folks pay per message) you've got to provide an immediate value to your customers with your SMS marketing.

Mobile carriers like Verizon and AT&T have strict rules and regulations about SMS marketing – for instance, people have to "opt-in" to your campaign by texting a certain word to a certain number (for example, "text 'business' to 56789.) This single opt-in prevents unscrupulous marketers from sending text message spam.

Lastly SMS marketing has been rated as one of the least trustworthy forms of advertising so be cautious and make sure SMS marketing or ads are a good fit.

Getting Started With SMS Marketing

Here are five tips to help you take the guesswork out of getting started with SMS Marketing:

1. *Keep it simple.* Notice a pattern with mobile marketing? Whether it's the

mobile web or SMS marketing, the space and size limitations necessitate simple, direct communication.

2. *Don't send a lot of texts.* People will opt out of your text messaging campaign quickly if you overload them. Never send more than one or two texts per month.

3. *Make sure each text message contains immediate value.* Your text messages should always revolve around a promotion, contest or discount with a strong call to action and plenty of built-in, time-sensitive urgency.

4. *Use a double opt-in.* To increase the quality of your leads, once someone has opted in to your text message list, send them a confirmation message to make sure they intended to do so. This shows respect for your customers and ensures you're compliant with all of the guidelines set forth by mobile carriers.

5. *Advertise your mobile subscription campaign across all your other channels.* Make sure customers can learn about your text message offers through your website,

newsletter, store lobby and everywhere else you conduct marketing operations.

Apps

Of course, one of the most prominent features of smartphones is their ability to run "apps." There are millions of apps available for a variety of platforms, running the gamut from games to calendars to widgets to news and more. Apps offer your business a single platform to promote products and services, offer discounts and coupon codes, enable customers to share their experiences with your business with friends online and through social media, and more. It can definitely be beneficial to a business to build an app; the question for most small businesses is whether the return on investment will bear out over the long run.

Unless you're a coder (programmer, developer, etc.), you won't be able to create your own app. You'll have to hire an app reseller, development firm or a freelance coder and designer to create it for you, and this is most likely not an insubstantial cost. Fold that into the cost of marketing both your app and brand (it takes quite a lot for an app to succeed in the marketplace – more than most small business owners can invest) and it doesn't make sense for most small businesses. For businesses on a tight budget getting an app from a reseller may be a more attractive alternative as apps may be leased or rented for a fraction the cost of developing an app.

Also, as HTML5 rises, and the functionality and feel of mobile pages comes closer to those of apps, it's becoming easier than ever to simply use a mobile-optimized site to help consumers connect with your business via their phones or tablets. Whether an app is developed or a mobile site is optimized the main question is what is the purpose of either.

Mobile Advertising

Much of the information contained in the previous chapter on Paid Search is applicable here, but there are some things you need to know about paid advertising as it applies on mobile sites. Of course, as with the chapter on Paid Search, this chapter assumes that you'll use Google Mobile Ads for your mobile advertising campaign, as it's the major player in the market right now. According to Statcounter.com Google had 88.1% of all mobile search as of October 2013. Search ads are the biggest part of the mobile advertising market, and you can set up an AdWords campaign that's specific to mobile (and only targets users with devices that have full web browsers.)

Mobile advertising comes with a lot of advantages – it's still fairly cheap (compared to desktop web prices,) and it's fast becoming more accepted among consumers, who resisted mobile advertising strongly at first. Here are four tips for making sure your business gets the most out of mobile advertising:

1. *Use a local mobile ad network.* Most small businesses rely on local traffic for their business, either as an intrinsic part of their business model, or because of natural customer preference for locally-based businesses. In order to capitalize on local traffic, it's best to use a local mobile ad network. An ad network is a company that connects advertisers to websites that want to host their ads. Essentially, they aggregate ad space supply and match it with advertiser demand, delivering ads to apps and mobile websites. There are many large-scale ad networks, but the one you want

is a local mobile ad network that shows your ads to users who are on their mobile devices searching for local information (such as a restaurant, a local service, etc.) The publishers on these networks are usually directory services, mapping and navigation apps, and so forth. Local advertising is more targeted, so it tends to be more expensive than general advertising, but it delivers better results over the long run. You can generally purchase advertising through a website or a direct-sales team, and select from Cost-Per-Click (CPC) advertising, Cost-Per-Action (CPA) advertising (e.g, pay per call, pay per store visit, pay per form filled out online, etc.) and Cost-Per-Impression advertising.

2. *Go to where your customers are.* Assuming you're a small business that depends on local traffic, you'll need to use a feature of ad networks called geo-targeting (or more recently talked about geo-fencing which can target ad recipients in areas measured in city blocks) so that only mobile users in certain zip codes will see your ads. However, if you've got a

small business with a wider reach (you can ship anywhere in the nation, or you run a business in a popular tourist destination, for instance) it makes sense to get involved with an ad network that advertises nationwide.

3. *Get a mobile landing page.* Sending customers to your home page might not be the right option – the best conversions come from well-optimized mobile landing pages. You can get started for free (for the first year) with Google Sites. Of course, your mobile landing page should link to your main site, but you want to use it to communicate the most important pieces of information about your business without clutter or complicating a user's navigations. Here are the three most important elements no mobile landing page should leave out:

   a) Your address, a map and a picture of your location, so customers can easily locate your physical business.

   b) Your phone number, hours of operation, and the region you serve.

c) Features that are relevant to your business and the pitch you made in your mobile ad, such as online appointment scheduling

4. *Ensure your conversion points are trackable and mobile-friendly.* As with any advertisement, you're trying to get consumers to take action – whether by becoming a customer or a qualified lead. When folks are on their smartphones, you've got a much smaller window to capture their attention and desire, and a much smaller margin of error, as well. Ensure that your conversion points are all mobile-friendly. You want to encourage your mobile audience to call you, Email you, give you some contact information (on a very short, simple form,) make an appointment, follow you on Facebook, etc. – but you need to make it devastatingly simple to do so, or you'll lose a large number of potential customers. You also have to make sure you're tracking your conversion rate so you can determine which mobile ads are performing and which ones need work.

QR Codes

QR Codes look similar to bar codes, and you may have seen them around town. They're a white square with a lot of squiggly black marks in the middle intended to be scanned by folks with smartphones.

For a while, QR codes were all the rage, but marketers slowly figured out that they're only effective for businesses with their own mobile app, mobile optimized website, or pure mobile website. As a small business, it's unlikely you've got an app (or that you should develop one) so QR codes are likely not a wise investment (see apps and resellers above for exceptions) .

If you do have an app, and you want to use QR codes to promote it, remember that you should place them sensibly: Don't put them on your mobile website or the back of a bus. Put them on promotional materials, business cards, posters, invoices, etc.; in other words, somewhere it makes sense for someone to pull out their phone and scan it.

Alternatives: Facebook Marketing

Facebook isn't just a great place to waste a few hours looking at friends' pictures and playing *Candy Crush*. It has actually come to function like a second Web within the Web. According to Statistic Brain, as of January 1, 2014, there were over 1.3 billion users on the site; if it were a nation, it would be the third largest in the world after China and India. And according to KISSmetrics, people share more than 30 billion pieces of content per month, including pictures, links, status updates, videos and more.

Facebook may be a great place to find your future customers, but then again it may not. Facebook is not Google and you would be ill advised to use the same tactics and strategies on Facebook as you do on Google. Unfortunately, most marketers and small businesses don't understand the unique ecosphere of the world's largest social media site, and end up wasting their precious budget on ineffective tactics. However if you target audience is on Facebook it can be a low cost highly effective way to reach that audience.

What's *truly* unfortunate about ineffective Facebook marketing is that it's may be so easy to put the world's largest social media platform to work for your business. Provided you've got a little familiarity with it (you've got a personal profile, for instance) this guide will get you started without a need for expansive technical understanding or any of the complicated add-ons floating around the Web.

Who Uses Facebook

There is a major (and widespread) misunderstanding out there that Facebook is something just for kids. It should be obvious that this isn't the case – after all, one-seventh of the world's population has a profile – but the myth somehow persists. Yes, the social media giant started as a social network for students at Harvard, where its founder, Mark Zuckerberg, went to college. But now the largest demographic segment of Facebook users happens to be folks between the ages of 35 and 54, and the fastest-growing segment is the 55-and-over crowd. So don't make the mistake of skipping Facebook marketing because you're targeting adults; you will definitely find them there.

The Three Main Facebook Marketing Tools

There are three separate tools Facebook offers to marketers (or anyone interested in using them) and each has its own advantages and disadvantages. However, combing all of them could maximize your effectiveness and reach.

1. Facebook Pages. Pages are like personal profiles for brands, businesses, organizations, products or celebrities/public figures. Unlike profiles, which have limitations on the numbers of friends someone can have and which require mutual relationships, anyone and everyone can "like" a Page. Pages are easy to set up and are free to do so. You can get started here.

2. Advertisements. Facebook has an advertising platform that can be highly targeted for demographics, geographic locations and even more specific consumer differentiators like occupation and what folks majored in back in college. Because Facebook also allows users input on the ads they see, their

targeting measures only get better with each passing day.

3. Facebook Groups. These are like online discussion forums, but they have some of the features of Pages and profiles built in. They are free to create and, once they're rolling, engender a high level of engagement – so long as you're willing to invest the time and energy it takes to curate the group and continually offer new and interesting content to keep the discussion going.

Marketing with Pages

Advertisements and groups are very effective, but the most widespread use of Facebook marketing by small businesses is through Pages because of their relative simplicity and low cost. Here is a list of best practices for marketing with a Page:

1. *Set up your "Info" Tab.* You wouldn't let your "About" page stay bank on your website, and it's poison to let your "Info" tab stay blank on your Facebook Fan Page. If people don't know who you are and what you do, they're going to click on the "Info" tab, so be sure

you've got the most important information listed here. It's best to write this specifically for Facebook in a friendly, casual, informal way (trying to keep it stylistically simpler to the social media vernacular) rather than copy-and-pasting it from your website. At the very least, it should incorporate the following:

a) *What your business does*

b) *Why your business is different*

c) *Interesting details*

2. *Use Custom Tabs.* Facebook has its own version of HTML that it calls FBML. It's structurally very simple to use and implement, and is a great way to create custom tabs featuring any content you would otherwise include in any other web page, including design, content or features. If you don't know how to code in HTML, you can skip this part, as Facebook makes it fairly easy to create a compelling Page without it, but it's an excellent differentiator to put to work for your small business.

3. *Set up different landing pages for different users.* This is where custom tabs come in handy. It's important to set up different landing pages for users with different statuses. For instance, for people that already "like" your page, you can direct them to a custom tab that offers them a special discount or promotion. For people that haven't yet done so, you can send them to a landing page that illustrates all the benefits of becoming a fan.

4. *Manage what you post carefully.* Any time you post to your wall, it may show up in the News Feed of anyone who has "liked" your page. This is a privilege, not a right! It's crucial not to spam people by posting things that aren't useful (or at least entertaining) to your fans. Be respectful of your audience and as with other types of Internet content make sure your posts are relevant and provide value to your reader. Also, keep in mind that the most heavily trafficked times of day are around 9 AM and 5 PM, so try to time your posts to coincide with those hours

in order to get as many eyeballs on your Page as possible.

5. *Keep people engaged.* People use social media in a fundamentally different way than they use search engines. When they are searching Google, they're looking for a solution to a problem, a product for a need or an answer to their question. They don't mind an advertiser offering their suggestion into the mix. However, when people are on Facebook, they're interested in playing games with friends, posting snarky comments, looking at photographs, and otherwise *being social.* Make sure that your Facebook marketing is done in the spirit of social media. Get your fans involved with your Page and offer them plenty of opportunities to engage and interact. Many companies ask their fans thought-provoking, open-ended questions related to their industry. Others solicit opinions on new projects and ideas for products or services. Still more run contests for their users with substantial, valuable prizes to create engagement. Whatever your tactic, be sure you're not just standing back with

an advertising megaphone blasting off impersonal marketing messages without interacting or attempting to inspire interaction with your fans.

6. *Use analytics to measure your results.* Facebook offers analytics for Pages that are quite useful. If you notice big movements (either up or down) in your number of Likes, for instance, you can take a look at what you've been posting recently (and how often) and analyze the trends to plan your future content releases. While the number of Likes is important keep a close watch on "talking about this" metric which measures interaction with or people touching your page in some way. An active page ("talking about this") is more important than a page with a lot of Likes and not many talking about it.

Using Targeted Advertising on Facebook

Facebook captures <u>a ton of standard demographic information</u> on its users. Its internal Data Science Team collects information on what its users "like," what music they listen to, what articles they read, what videos they watch, how long they sit through advertisements, and much more.

Because of this, Facebook has a treasure trove of information about consumer behavior, and much of it is available to businesses looking to advertise on the site. Just about anything available on their profile is available for you to target – and track.

You can purchase CPM or CPC advertising on Facebook. Like Google, Facebook will also provide you with information on the current market price of bids on ads similar to your own, and you can set a daily limit on how many ads are shown so you don't accidentally go over your budget.

Here are four things you need to know about advertising on Facebook:

1. *There are several ad subtypes to choose from.* Some ads will direct people to your Page, and others will send them to an off-Facebook landing page. There are ads you can create to promote a Facebook event, and ads to send people to Facebook Groups and apps, as well. There are ads to promote the post you make on your Page which some say are

the most effective of all types, but the key decision again is what is your purpose? Sidebar ads are better for Likes while promoting a post is better for engagement. The question is what do you want to accomplish.

2. *Facebook users can rate or delete your ads.* Unless you're running an ad promoting an event, your ads include a "like" button. When people "like" your ad, it makes your ad more effective, because Facebook will show users' friends what ads they've "liked," conferring all-important social proof on your marketing efforts. If someone likes an ad pointing to your Page, they'll automatically be enrolled as a fan and start receiving your updates in their News Feeds. Of course, this is a double-edged sword, because if people don't like your ads, they can close you off from advertising to them again. The one silver lining here is that FB asks them to provide information about why they didn't want to see the ad, which can arm you with the knowledge you need to improve your ads or refine your strategy.

3. *You have formidable options for targeting.* If you are a local business or location you can target folks by location. Want to target fans of your local sports team? You can do that. Want to target people who have liked your competitions Page? You can do that with special software (and rest assured that your competition can do that as well.) Want to target the members of a group or people who have commented on or Liked a Page? You can do that. Keep in mind the first order of business in an ad campaign is defining and identifying your audience. Understand their demographic first and *then* use Facebook's targeting options. Until you know as close as possible your target audience demographic the best targeting tools Facebook has will do more to waste money than drive traffic and sales. Finding your target audience and creating a "custom audience" for your Facebook ads is in our opinion is the most effective way to target your ads.

4. *You have powerful options for custom-tailoring your ads.* You don't have to send out the same copy to different target markets.

You can send different ads to different segments of the market, and you should – the better targeted your ads are, the better click through rate you'll see (refer to A/B testing in the chapter on PPC ads). For instance, if you were targeting fans of the local sports team (as in the previous example) you might write a sports-specific ad and then have that shown only to folks who've got the team in the Likes & Interest portion of their page.

Marketing with Facebook Groups

Groups offer more community-building than Pages. Facebook groups tend to be used less for commercial purposes – and people will tolerate a lot less in the way of marketing – but they can still be put to good use. Groups tend to have smaller user bases than Pages, but if properly cultivated, they elicit a much higher level of participation and engagement from users.

Here are four things you need to know about marketing with Facebook Groups:

1. Pages are for businesses, products, etc. as described above. Groups are for

industries, niches, consumers of a product or service, and really groups of any kind. Don't create a group for your company, create a group for the consumers that your company serves, then offer them useful, valuable content and discussion that regularly goes outside the scope of your business. The trick here is not to directly market your business to users, but to establish yourself as a trusted authority in the niche.

2. The primary strength of Groups is creating discussion. Any Facebook Group that's successful has plenty of active, spirited discussion. Remember, Groups are like online forums, but they tend to be more disorganized, because anyone can start a thread and anyone can comment. This means that if a user starts a discussion, you've got to get into the fray quickly with open-ended comments designed to create more discussion – regardless of whether that discussion is negative or positive. Any tactics you used designed to shut down free debate will have a chilling effect on the rest of the conversations in your

Group, so ensure that you're dealing constructively with not just your enthusiastic customers, but your strident critics, as well.

3. Use best practices for Group messages. You can send out bulk messages to members of your Group, just like Email, but people generally don't respond positively to this if you're using it in the same fashion as Email marketing. If you don't have anything that's actually substantial and useful for folks to see in their inboxes (such as truly worthwhile discounts, coupons and promotions) don't send it out. Also, be sure not to send out a group message too often and how often that is depends on the group, use good judgment and don't spam. It's much less intrusive and invasive to post offers and promotions to the Group wall, and you'll likely get a better reception from marketing-fatigued consumers.

4. Get in the fray and stay there. A group without engagement fizzles quickly. Though it can be time-consuming to keep up with all of the conversations in your Group, it's worth the investment

of your time (or worth hiring a social media marketing manager to do it for you) if you've got hundreds or thousands of people regularly interacting. Alternatively, you can go and get involved in Facebook Groups that are already established (and relevant to your company's industry or niche) but here you'll have to be even more strident about refraining from spam. Most Groups are strict about not spamming, and it's easy to get kicked out if you're advertising and not substantively contributing to discussions. Some Groups do allow certain types of marketing, but it's important to read their About pages or contact the Group's administrator before posting. Even content marketing can get you in trouble here, so make sure you're operating by the rules of the Group or you run the risk of alienating a large number of otherwise potential customers.

A parting thought (and warning) on Facebook Marketing

Before anything else determine if you target audience or market is on or can be reached using Facebook. If they are not then there is no business reason to use Facebook (or any other social network). If they are on Facebook then there are few business reasons not to go there.

Alternatives: Email Marketing

There was a time when Email was frowned upon and considered impersonal. Now it's a common form of communication. Almost everyone has an Email address even if they don't have a computer, especially as smartphone ownership becomes even more mainstream and commonplace.

Not only do people have Email addresses, they actively use them. In fact, 91% of consumers check their Email at least once a day. So if you want to find a way to get your business in front of people, contacting them by Email is an almost foolproof way to do that. The key is to find a way to entice them to give you their Email address.

It's not as tough as it may seem. While many people hold their Email address near and dear, they are fairly open to sharing it if they want to know about your company's products and/or services. You have to peak their interest in a meaningful way.

The best way to do this is by giving them something. Since most people recognize that giving a business their Email address means they will receive solicitations and marketing information, if you offer them something of value, they are more inclined to give it to you. Don't worry, giving customers something in exchange for their Email address really helps set up your relationship as a commercial one that includes commerce and the selling or products or services.

What could you possibly offer your potential customers?

You have lots of wonderful information and knowledge to offer. If you package it in a way that is interesting but informative, your customers will take it and appreciate you for giving it to them. By creating content like eBooks, video workshops, webinars, discounts on services and free consulting you have something of high perceived value to share.

That's the most important thing you must keep in mind when you are creating any kind of content whether you share it in exchange for Email addresses or money—it must be of high perceived value.

What does "high perceived value" mean?

You have to strike a balance between giving away something worthwhile and giving away the whole kit and caboodle. This is why research is important before you begin creating anything to use in an Email marketing campaign. You have to determine what your audience wants to know. Once you figured that out you can tell them. That's how you make something of high perceived value.

Focus on one main concept that allows you to demonstrate your expertise while solving a problem. Once you've done that, you're ready to begin your Email marketing campaign.

How to get started?

You should always create the content first. This will probably take some time and should be completed before you set up your campaign. But once your content is created and ready to be shared, you have to get the proper tools. Email marketing is so valuable that there are companies that have created tools to make the process very seamless and fairly easy to set up. It's just a matter of choosing the one that works best for you.

Here are some of the more popular Email marketing tools to help you get started with your research. I don't get any type of income from sharing these links. They're a good starting point for tools you can use.

1. Aweber

2. Mailchimp

3. GetResponse (we use)

4. MyEmma

5. iContact (we use)

These are just a few of the tools available but if you've never done Email

marketing or haven't taken the time to really consider it, you need to familiarize yourself with how they work. One thing you could do is find out which tool is most commonly used in your particular industry. That research could help with your decision making process. Most offer a free trial, so give one a test drive.

What's next?

When you've chosen the Email marketing tool you want to use, take some time and get acquainted with how it works while setting up your Email messages. Most provider offer video training in addition to full featured documentation. There are typically three to four different Email messages you should compose to move people through your sales funnel.

1. Opt-In Email

2. Once someone gives you their Email address, they'll receive a confirmation message. This is where they make the decision to actually be on your Email list. It's called a double opt-in because it gives people the ability not to just be added to Email lists without their permission. It's an additional layer of security for consumers. Since it comes as soon as the person gives their Email address, you don't have to worry about them forgetting about it. And with a double opt-in delivery rates are usually higher.

3. Welcome/Introductory Email

4. This is your opportunity to share the content and officially introduce yourself to your new warm lead. You

may also include a download link for the free content. It's important that you share the content here and not sooner because you actually want the Emails in your marketing funnel. This message comes after the Email is truly confirmed. Always be adding to your Email list.

5. Marketing Email

6. This Email should come fairly soon after the welcome Email. Don't let people be a part of your Email list without some kind of marketing contact in the first couple of weeks of joining. You don't have to give anything away but you should look for ways to provide value. Share some kind of information or insight in this Email and include a call to action that relates to your business. Provide updates about new products you're offering, tidbits about the industry you're in or share more content you've created in these follow up Emails. This should be done consistently enough to keep your company fresh in customer's minds but not so often that they unsubscribe from your Email list.

How often should you contact your list?

This is a tough question to answer exactly. Unfortunately my answer is almost always, "It depends on your list". Start by sending Emails once a week then try experimenting with sending them more often or less often. You'll have to do some testing to see what causes people to abruptly unsubscribe. Just because you get one unsubscribe request doesn't mean that what you're doing isn't working. You have to look for patterns. This is definitely an ongoing process that you will be managing consistently. The longer you do it, the easier it will become but it's not something you can just set and forget. As with any active lead generation and lead management, you have to keep doing it while making tweaks along the way when necessary. For example; opt-out rates of less than 1% are usually irrelevant. However depending on the quality of your list that can be much higher.

Keeping Email marketing going

Once you've set up your Email marketing campaign and have sent out your first set of Emails, it's important that you put a plan in place for how you will continue to communicate with your Email list. In addition, you need to determine how long you will let your campaigns run and when they will be re-done.

It's best that you let your campaigns run for at least three months, especially when you're just starting out. That will give you some time to see how well it works and where you may need to iron out any kinks. Don't try to rush this process. You need to give it time to marinate properly and really provide you some benefit.

You could let it run for longer than three months but try to keep it between three to six months. You don't want to forget about it. Email marketing is a process that needs to be consistently massaged and updated to remain effective. But it is effective and should be a part of any Internet marketing campaign.

A Couple of Tips

An Email list of 10,000 that you do not interact with regularly I consider cold and most likely will not convert (buy something) well. An Email list of 1,000 that I interact with on a regular basis I consider warm and they most likely will convert better than a cold list. Keep your list warm.

You may have heard (or will hear) that Email marketing is dead. Just to be clear it is not even tired. Email marking campaigns run consistently that provide value to your list is one of the most effective online marketing channels that I have seen. We use it all the time, and it works.

Alternatives: Google+ Business

According to Google, <u>97% of its users search for local businesses online</u>, and <u>20% of every search is related to a location</u>. That means people aren't just searching for "clothing stores," they're searching for "clothing stores in Boston" or "tailors in Phoenix." In order to facilitate these one-in-five searches, the company launched Google Places for Business, an advanced search facility that is perfect for small businesses who are trying to target local customers rather than everyone on the World Wide Web.

This chapter can be confusing so please read the entire chapter or at least skip to the bottom for hopefully a simpler explanation.

History of Google Places for Business

Before we can dive into the different elements of Google Places for Business and how it relates to Google+ Business, here's a short (very recent) history lesson.

Initially this service was just called Google Places. It served as a way for businesses to take advantage of Google Maps. Rather than just waiting for Google to index your business and add it to Google Maps, Google Places gave you the power to create your listing to make it work best for you.

Google Places, at its most basic, allowed your business to get a listing on Google Maps so that it's easy for folks to find you (and use Maps to get directions to your business, or use their smartphones to navigate to you). This means that when a customer goes looking for "clothing stores in Boston," your web page won't just pop up in the organic SERP; it will also come up on a Maps section indented from the left of the organic web listings and, **this is huge**, position at the top of page 1 of the SERP. This is an excellent way to get your business on the Web with a small amount of effort, and immediately begin to create brand awareness and drive local sales. In short Google is giving all local business it can find a one page website and giving that website preferential treatment above all other websites and web pages.

As Google continued to grow and change, other tools were created to provide even more value to businesses. But Google Places was such a valuable tool that Google chose to roll it into another service that was launched called Google+ Business which gives businesses access to Google's social media community, Google+.

What is Google+?

Before we dive into how to use Google+ Business, it's important to discuss one of Google's products, Google+ (pronounced "Google Plus"). Launched in 2011, Google+ was created to add a social layer on top of Google's online properties like Gmail and Youtube that are already being used by millions of people. In an effort to take advantage of the social era of online communities, Google added a social networking element that gives users the ability to manage the information they share with their networks or "circles". Anyone who has a profile on one of Google's properties automatically has a Google+ page that just needs to be activated to use. Because of this, Google+ experienced rapid growth and is now considered one of the top social networking websites.

Why Google+ Business?

As with other social networking websites, Google+ has a version that allows businesses to take advantage of the service. It takes the value of Google Places and includes social networking features to create Google+ Business. So yes it's possible for you to simply create a Google Places page to make your business appear on Google Maps. However, Google+ Business makes it possible for you to galvanize the Google community in a much more meaningful way. While a Google+ account can be thought of as a Facebook account a Google+ Business listing can be thought of as a Facebook Page. There are differences but that is how I look at them.

When you create a Google Places account, your profile automatically looks like a basic Google+ profile. But in order to take full advantage of the social features of Google+, you have to sign up for Google+ Business. Once you do that, you have the ability to take advantage of all of the benefits of having a Google+ account with the added benefits of Google Places and Google+ Local.

Google+ Local is a consumer based service that makes it possible for people to discover businesses in their area based on Google searches they may do. It allows them to see places that people in their social media network have found as well as shows customer reviews for the businesses. By creating your account on Google Places, it gives you access to the Google+ Local network and all of the benefits of having a Google+ Business account.

Here are some of those benefits:

1. *Google is the new Yellow Pages.* When the Internet exploded, one of the first casualties was the old phonebook, at least among younger consumers and in urban areas with a high rate of Internet adoption. But using Google to find a local business wasn't as easy in the old days as it is now, and Google's express purpose for Google Places is to create a comprehensive replacement for that phonebook. Even in rural areas and places without heavy Internet use, Google Places is an excellent replacement for – or at the very least, complement to – the Yellow Pages. Even if you don't have a website, you

can make all of your pertinent information accessible to local customers at the click of a button.

2. *It helps your SEO efforts.* Since Google Places focuses on local search, there are fewer competitors jostling elbows with you for the top spot. Google Places restricts listings to businesses that are truly local to a given locality – not just the city, region or state that you serve. This gives you a much better chance to hit the top of the SERP for your location and category. And while this will not last, most local businesses that I talk to don't even know about this yet.

3. *It makes your business easy to find.* The Maps functionality gives customers your exact location, and is especially important to mobile customers, who are often looking for products and services while remaining on the go. This puts the power and reach of the widely popular Google Maps app (available across many platforms and devices) to work for your business.

4. *It's cost-effective.* Well, it's free, for that matter. And free is a much better price

than you would otherwise pay for a billboard ad or a spot on radio or television. Since small businesses need to maximize their reach for a minimal budget, taking the time to set up and claim your Google Places listing is a no-brainer. The same goes for expanding that profile to a Google+ Business one. This one is, again, huge.

5. *You are allowed to share status updates with customers.* Your Google+ Business profile includes a social feed that you can use to communicate with potential customers. This is the perfect place to share offers, business news and interesting updates about your company. These updates will be shared with everyone that's in your network. You will be able to actively encourage customers to share reviews, start conversations and spruce up your profile with a company logo and other images.

Your Google+ Business page will not only create a presence for your

Business that will show up in one of the most popular search engines, it will allow you to control how that presence represents your business.

Getting Started With Google+ Business

It's easiest to start by creating a <u>Google Places</u> account. The best part is that it's a completely free service. You may already have a Google Places listing and not know it – Google already indexes many businesses as part of its Maps functionality. Plus if you have a Gmail, Youtube or other Google account for your business, you already have a basic Google+ page.

However, if they've indexed you but you haven't signed up or you haven't activated your Google+ page, you don't have control over your Google Places listing and you're not getting the most out of the service.

Because there are multiple ways to go about setting up this account, you should choose one path. These are the best steps to follow to ensure that you don't accidentally set up multiple business accounts.

1. Create a Google Places Account

2. Click on the link to <u>Google Places for Business</u>

3. Click "Get Started for Free" when you get to the page

4. Type your business name in the search bar

5. If your business is already indexed, it will come up. If not, you'll be asked to input the information.

6. Submit your information

7. Choose how you want your information to be verified. It will either be by phone or mail.

8. Wait up to two weeks for the verification process to be complete.

9. Your account will be complete

Author's note: As fast as Google changes its web properties there is a good chance that by the time you read this it will have changed at least a little. If that is the case just Google "create a google places account" or go to our website for an update to this chapter. <u>http://www.mediamarketexperts.com/category/internet-marketing-book-updates/</u>

1. Create a Google+ Business Account

2. If you already have a personal Google+ account, don't use that one for your business page. Make sure you create a separate business account. It will be much easier to manage it if you go this route rather than trying to do everything under one account.

3. Visit the Google+ Business page

4. Click "Get Your Page"

5. Choose the type of organization that you have

6. Create a name for your page

7. Provide your website (if you have one)

8. Choose the type of audience that your business has

9. Customize your new Google+ Business page

Author's note: As fast as Google changes its web properties there is a good chance that by the time you read this it will have changed at least a little. If that is the case just Google "create a google+ business account" or go to

our website for an update to this chapter.
http://www.mediamarketexperts.com/catego
ry/internet-marketing-book-updates/

How to Get The Most Out Of Google+ Business

Here are eight ways you can optimize your Google+ Business listings:

1. *Be authentic about your business categories.* This is the number one mistake businesses make with their Google Places listing: They think they'll show up in searches more often by adding dozens of categories of products or services. Just because you can doesn't mean you should! In fact, your ranking will suffer if you category-stuff. Pick one – yes, *one* – category that suits your business best, and use that.

2. *Use a solid keyword strategy.* Just as you learned in the chapter on SEO, it's important to use relevant keywords to create good product or service descriptions that will entice customers to visit your location. In other words, write the information about your business as though it were a blog post,

and be sure to fill out every information box or your business won't appear in searches. When writing your business description, however, don't forget that we now live in a post-Hummingbird world, where keyword-stuffing will dramatically lower your rankings! Quality trumps quantity.

3. *Don't use cliché copy.* Every business "proudly serves" its customers and thinks it's "the best in town." You've got to work hard to differentiate your listing, and one of the best ways to do this is to use humor. Let a little of your personality shine through in your copy and people will feel a connection that will compel them to visit you over your competitors who are featuring scrubbed, robotic, hackneyed copy.

4. *List your phone number correctly.* That's not a "Captain Obvious" tip – that's a major mistake that a lot of businesses make in their Google Places listing. Some leave their phone number out entirely, some give the incorrect one, and the biggest sin of all is posting your phone number in a format that Google bots can't read

when they're crawling and looking for indexing information. That means your phone number needs to be in a text field – not in a picture format.

5. *Use images and videos.* You can spruce up your Google+ Business profile by adding information about your business, a cover photo and a logo. You can also share videos and other images in your social feed. When someone is searching for a business like yours, they will gain a lot of insight into your business but also the people that support it, especially if your images and videos are high-quality. It's important to note here that branding is very important on Google+ Business. Whatever logos and images you're using on your storefront, website and other promotional materials need to also go on your profile page. Google has a service called Google Business Photos. This gives potential customers a 360-degree view of the interior of your shop, and the photographs are taken by trusted Google photographers. You can use Google Business Photos to differentiate your business by giving folks a sneak peek at the space (and the

way) in which you do business. Of course, it goes without saying that your business space should be squeaky clean the day the photographers show up! Business Photos is still pretty young – it was launched in May 2013 – and there are some businesses holding out to see whether Google can find a way to make it scalable on a national basis, but it could lead to great things for your business if it's offered in your area. It's always best, after all, to give people the most information possible as they're deciding on which business to purchase products and services from. You can sign up for Google Business Photos here.

6. *Make sure all of your locations are on Google Places.* If you have more than one branch of location, ensure you've got each location's address and phone number registered with Google Places. If you only have one branch, but you offer services in different areas, make sure your page has all of your service areas listed.

7. *Ask people to review you on Google Places.*
We'll cover reviews more thoroughly in
a later chapter, but it never hurts to ask
customers who are pleased with your
products and services to rate you on
Google Places. Obviously, the greater
number you have of positive reviews,
the more social proof your business has
– and the more business you'll
ultimately attract. One caveat: Don't
attempt to rate or review your own
business, or try to get others to do so
dishonestly. Google has sophisticated
algorithms set up to determine whether
ratings are real or disingenuous, and
"stuffing" your ratings can sink your
rank on the SERP quickly.

8. *Tie Google+ Business in with your other
marketing efforts.* In other words, make
sure your website, Facebook Page,
social media offerings and content
marketing efforts contain a link of some
kind to your Google+ Business listing.
This will help you improve your online
visibility and expand your community.

The Future of Google+ Business

Google+ has hundreds of millions of users, it is being incorporated into all aspects of Google. Google+ Business listings now come up in Google SERPs right along with other websites and above most websites. It's become a natural part of the search process so as long as your business is relevant to the search (which it will be) interested individuals will click on the link to your page. This provides a lot of value in bringing organic search your way. By including your website on your Google+ Business page, you can help target that traffic even further.

The socializing of Google products will really help connect your brand across one that is well known around the world. The added bonus is that most of these features are 100% free! If you aren't taking full advantage of everything Google has to offer you and your business, you should definitely start right now.

In closing this is the most confusing chapter in the book because of the evolution of Google's social properties and how they rolled them into the business world. So here is my attempt to simplify in as few words as I can think of.

Google+: Google's social network and the equivalent of a Facebook account or personal profile.

Google Places: A local listing Google provides businesses similar to an online Yellow Pages listing or Yelp listing.

Google+ Local: A kind of local search engine inside of Google's search engine that focuses on local listings (see Google Places).

Google+ Business: A business listing that used to be and kind of still is Google Places and Google Places for Business. And is somewhat the equivalent of a Facebook Page.

If this hurts your head like it does mine sometimes don't fret. Go create or claim your Google Places listing and create your Google+ Business listing. It will be the best thing you can do for your local business' online presence.

Alternatives: Managing and Marketing Your Online Reputation

The Internet has changed the way that word-of-mouth marketing works. The old rule was that every person in the world knew about 250 people, and so a satisfied customer (theoretically) could spread positive word about your business within that reach. Nowadays, with sites like Yelp, Google+ Business (with its built-in review functionality), Angie's List, Insider Pages, and more, the world of word of mouth has been up-ended. All of these sites are one-stop platforms where potential customers can search for a local business, and also read reviews and critiques of its performance.

In fact, a recent survey showed that 8 out of 10 Americans agreed that online reviews influenced their purchasing behavior. According to Nielsen, consumer opinions posted online are the most trusted form of advertising and second only to recommendations from people known to the prospect. Go to the URL below for an InfoGraphic and more information.

https://www.google.com/search?q=nielse
n+global+trust+in+advertising+survey+info
graphic

On top of that, if someone has a bad experience with a business, they'll likely take to Facebook or Twitter, in addition to the review sites mentioned above, to complain about it, or even post something on a blog. Regardless of whether you see it as the tyranny of the mob or the wisdom of the crowds, you can't ignore it.

Everyone's a Critic

It's critical that you know how your brand is perceived in the digital sphere, because your online reputation – which is made up of what customers share with each other about you – can be the deciding factor between wild success and shuttering the windows.

In order to manage and market your online reputation, you'll need to learn a new set of skills, including keeping an ear to the ground (metaphorically) to know what people are saying about your business on the Internet, engaging with your customers on social media, and promoting yourself on the most effective channels. It's not enough to sit back and hope that all is well – managing and marketing your online reputation is a matter of life or death.

A successful reputation strategy is made up of three components: Scrutinizing, Supervising and Reputation Marketing.

Scrutinizing Your Online Reputation

There are as many opinions out there as there are customers – and there is no shortage of platforms available to folks who want to air out those opinions. In order to get a handle on what folks are saying (or not saying) about your business, you've got to get tuned in.

The first step is Googling yourself. You should be doing this on a regular basis anyway, to see how your SEO is performing. But ask yourself a different set of questions this time: What's the first impression people are getting of your site? Is your online presence well-maintained and up to date? Is your business coming up in online forums or on blogs? What's the first, second and third listings for your site? The purpose here is to try and figure out what your customer sees when they Google your business's name –

remember, one in five of every Google search is local!

Next check out popular review and community sites out there. Yelp, CitySearch, Yahoo! Local, Amazon, Angie's List, TripAdvisor, OpenTable, Epinions, Insider Pages and more. It's important to know who's got the biggest megaphones – and where your potential customers might get potential negative information from.

Once you have a sense of what folks are saying about you, set up a Google Alert with your business's name. Any time a review, publication, or blog (but usually not a comment or social media post) goes up on the Web, Google will let you know. Many sites also allow you to sign up to receive an alert whenever a comment is posted about you. Lastly, you can keep an eye on what folks are tweeting about your business by going to search.twitter.com or using a tool like TweetDeck.

Supervising

It's easy to figure out what people are saying. It's a lot harder to influence that conversation.

Of course, you should already have claimed your listing on Google+ Business, because it's free. But other sites like Foursquare, Bing and Yelp also have listings for your business, and you can usually claim them and optimize them for free (though some sites offer premium functionality for an additional fee.)

Once you've got your listings claimed, it's time to get into the fray and start responding to customer reviews. You've got to be very careful here, however! This is a precarious position to be in, and requires deft handling and strong customer relations skills.

Responding to Negative Reviews

Of course, it's easy to show your gratitude for people who leave you positive reviews. In fact, you don't even have to respond to every positive review, especially if the overall majority of comments out in the digital sphere are positive.

However, you can never let a negative review go unanswered. In order to effectively manage your online reputation, you have to be seen as someone who can take input, take useful steps to resolve the conflict and mollify the upset customer, and be gracious while doing so. But it can be difficult to maintain your cool when someone leaves a sarcastic or downright hurtful review about your business.

There's a theory called the online disinhibition effect that states many people will abandon social restrictions on the Internet they would otherwise normally adhere to in a face-to-face conversation. You've seen this – "trolls" on the Internet say awful, racist, explicit things on a regular basis for no reason other than the fact that they have anonymity and an audience. Because there is no meaningful reprisal for saying something nasty (maybe they get kicked out of a forum or site and simply re-register with another username,) some customers will take an experience that was barely negative and turn it into a scathing tirade on your business that is completely out of proportion. The painter Goya was right: "The sleep of reason products monsters."

It can be hard to keep your wits about you – after all, someone is negatively reviewing your business, often without knowing what they're talking about or without having complete information, often without any forgiveness for normal human mistakes, and often without mercy. Your business is how

you feed your family and make your living!
How can you not take it personally?

The worst thing you can do, to employ an
Internet-ism, is "feed the trolls." If your
blood is boiling, take a break and cool
yourself down. There are only two ways to
control negative reviews: Up your
performance, and respond graciously. If you
feel hurt or angry and respond in kind, anyone
happening upon the conversation will
(justifiably) only get a worse opinion of you
and your business.

You've got to respond publicly. However, you
don't have to do so right away. Many
business owners have found that sending a
polite, private message to the hostile
commenter offering to "fix" their problems
will so impress the critic that they go right
back into the site and either delete or edit
their negative comment. Try this first!
Regardless of whether you get a response, you
need to make a public comment. If you've
communicated with them and they've taken
you up on your offer to fix the problem they
had with your business, you can leave a
comment after theirs referencing this. Try
something like, "I'm so glad we were able to

work out a way to fix your unsatisfactory experience, and I'm looking forward to the opportunity you gave me to make it right." An apology and some humility go a long way – after all, the buying public understands that we all make mistakes, but most of us aren't willing to forgive someone who's unrepentant in the first place. If you can't reach the user by private message, either because you have no way to reach them, or they don't respond, simply leave a comment offering to make everything right for them on their next visit, and including a sincere apology.

Being Authentic

Never, ever, ever post a fake review about your own business. Never post a fake review about your competition, either. If you're trying to "fluff" yourself up or take someone else down, you might get away with it once, sure. But the risk compared to the reward is way out of proportion. This is a practice called "shilling" and it can be a major embarrassment for your company. If people find out you're using dishonest tactics to market your business, they're going to assume you'll be dishonest in doing business with them, as well – and trust is the foundation of any business relationships.

One form of shilling, known as "astroturfing," can also come with legal fines – for instance, the New York State Attorney General's office fined a cosmetic surgery clinic $300,000 in civil penalties after they discovered employees were posing as "satisfied customers" writing positive reviews.

Truth be told, if you're doing your job and doing it well – and going the extra mile for each and every customer – they'll be motivated to write positive reviews of your company.

Using Negative Reviews for Positive Effect

You can usually tell who's being a troll (or who your competitors are) because there isn't anything useful or actionable in their comments. People are generally good, and want businesses (especially small businesses) to succeed. If someone posts a negative review about your business, read it carefully to figure out where you upset them. If you start to see patterns emerging in the reviews, it's time to start experimenting with and iterating the way you do business in order to make it a better experience for folks coming through the door.

Reputation Marketing

Once you know what people are saying and you're out there in the fray, managing negative comments and encouraging positive reviews, it's time to up your game by promoting your good name which is where Reputation Marketing comes in.

Reputation Marketing in its simplest form is an idea where you recruit or ask for positive reviews from satisfied customers and promote them where appropriate, like your website. If you see a satisfied customer as they are leaving after a purchase ask for a review on Google, Yelp, Insider Pages, etc.

Reputation Marketing includes but is not limited to:

- Training staff to check with customers as they are leaving

- Asking for reviews when a customer has a positive experience

- Collecting and posting positive reviews on your website

153

- Providing customers automated means to leave reviews

- Using those positive reviews in your other marketing channels

And remember NEVER pay for or give incentives for reviews. If you are going the extra mile for your customers you should not have to.

As you consistently collect and promote positive 5 star reviews any negative reviews will be pushed off the first page where your reviews are listed. As well as your average review score will go up.

Consider the tale of 2 hypothetical children's dentists. Good Reputation Dentist ranks well on the search results pages, has 15 reviews and a 4.5 star rating in Google. All of reviews on page 1 of the review page are recent and highly recommend the dentist for children. Bad Reputation Dentist also ranks well on the search results pages, has 5 reviews and a 2.5 star rating in Google. The reviews on page 1 of the review page are more than a year old and do not recommend the dentist for children. Which one would you consider taking your children to (or recommending for other's children)?

It used to be not so long ago that ranking high in the SERPs alone was enough of a strategy to drive traffic and customers to a business. Not any longer. Within the last 2 years reputation and its close cousin, authority, have become the currency of the Internet. As the commercial says, what's in your wallet?

Not convinced? Then check out this Yelp.com study reported in the Huffington Post that found a causal relationship between a 1/2 a star (3.5 and 4 stars) and 19% higher sales:
http://www.huffingtonpost.com/2012/09/0 6/yelp-study-ratings-restaurant-reservations_n_1861720.html

Once you start making yourself known in the online community that's already talking about you, you'll find your business gaining more traction. After all, the conversation is going to happen – whether you're a part of it or not! You might as well be out there scrutinizing, supervising and marketing your relationship.

Section 3: The Solutions

Solutions: Putting It All Together

Building websites, paying for search, using Facebook, marketing your online reputation…it's a dizzying, bewildering array of actions to take, and it can baffle the most dedicated small business owner. After all, corporations have entire departments devoted to online marketing – how are you supposed to do the work of ten people?

Luckily, you don't have to.

You *do* have to invest time and resources into Internet marketing, but it would be crazy to think you had to personally plan, execute and manage a strategy that included every tactic in this book. Rather, you've got to figure out what strategy makes sense for your business, find out where you're getting results, and focus your efforts there. In other words, you're looking for the strategy where the Pareto Principle holds true: What is the vital few and what is the trivial many? 20% of something is always responsible for 80% of your results, so you've got to spend 80% of your valuable time managing that 20%.

In the case of Internet Marketing for small businesses, this means taking care of the fundamentals first: Building a website – *every small business owner must build a website* – and managing your online reputation on review sites like Yelp and Foursquare as well as marketing your online reputation by facilitating 5 star reviews. Beyond that, it usually means picking two of the "alternatives" that are expounded on in detail in the previous chapters. Maybe that's SEO and PPC, maybe that's Facebook and content marketing, maybe that's Google+ Business and mobile marketing. Which ones you choose depends on what makes sense for your business and your budget. And this is HUGE, it depends on *where your target market is*. It's important to note – you may not pick *only* two, but you do have to choose where to *focus*.

How to Build an Effective Internet Marketing Plan

How do you know which approach makes sense for your business? By building a planned, organized Internet marketing campaign that keeps things simple and can be implemented immediately. "He who fails to plan is planning to fail" - Winston Churchill during World War II (as near as we can tell)

There are five steps:

1. *Define your customer.* You should be able to give a snap definition of your products or your business to anyone who asks. But can you give a snap definition of your customers? In order to do that, you've got to be honest with yourself and answer this question: What does the ideal customer look like?

   - *Are they male or female? How old are they?*

   - *Where do they work and what do they do?*

   - *What is their job profile? Are they entrepreneurs, executives, managers, workers?*

   - *What is their education level? High school? Bachelor's? Master's?*

   - *How often do they need my product or service? How often can they afford it?*

- *How do they use my product? What problem do they have that I'm helping them solve?*

- *How much time do they spend on the Internet? What do they spend their time doing while on the Internet? How do they access the Internet – through mobile or desktop?*

- Once you've got this information, you'll be able to build a profile of that customer – and start figuring out how to reach them. For instance, if you're primarily marketing to a 55-and-over crowd, it's not going to make sense to start a mobile marketing campaign, because 55 year-olds don't send and receive text messages as often as younger people. And if you're trying to reach teenagers, using content marketing to offer them a bunch of white papers, spreadsheets and PowerPoint presentations might not get you where you want to be.

2. *Pick your targets.* Where are you going to focus your efforts? It's best to try and

choose complementary approaches. For instance, PPC is *only* a complementary approach, and it works very well with SEO. Facebook marketing can be great, and it's even better when paired with content marketing. You'll want to use you resources in channels that have a high potential for cross-promotion and message reinforcement. But times change and audiences move, so if you find in your research that a substantial portion of your target audience is migrating to another platform or using a specific website, consider the following before choosing what marketing channel to use:

- *How much traffic does a channel get?*

- *Can you verify with some certainty your target audience can be reached via the channel?*

- *How well does the content place on search engines?*

- *Do you already have competitors there?*

- *This is not necessarily a bad thing, if your competitors are there then there is a good chance so is your audience.*

- *If there are competitors, how heavy is the competition?*

- *If it will cost you more than you can earn look for other channels where this is not the case.*

- *What are the PPC costs (if any) in the channel?*

   a) *Low PPC costs could mean low competition but also low opportunity.*

   b) *High PPC costs could mean a lot of opportunity but is it worth it? Are they other more effective channels?*

   These are all excellent clues that will help you measure whether or not a channel will bear fruit. One of our favorite tools to analyze demographics of website visitors (which can be very helpful) is www.quantcast.com.

3. *Set your budget.* Too many small business owners make the mistake of starting

with a budget and attempting to write the marketing plan within that parameter. But you can actually get a better picture of what costs will be involved by starting the marketing plan first, then tailoring it to meet your budget needs. Think big! Design your ideal marketing plan first, then put a goal-oriented set of steps in motion to eventually reach it. You probably already have an idea of how much you're willing (or able) to spend, and your ideal marketing plan will likely exceed that, but it will help you refine your priorities to get the most exposure and results for the money you've got to spend. Remember, as your marketing strategy starts to pull in results, you'll increase your sales. So as long as you've got a plan, you can keep expanding your campaign until you're striving on all the fronts with as much energy as you can dream of. If you're using PPC, it's important to check in daily for the first two weeks to make sure you're paying for advertising that's getting you results. You can also get involved with an ad exchange by swapping newsletter or banner ads with other sites who are

budget-conscious and looking to
expand their marketing.

4. *Create your content.* If you're looking to
   do content marketing, now is the time
   to start producing those blog posts,
   videos and InfoGraphics. If you're
   looking to do PPC, now is the time to
   start writing engaging, compelling copy.
   If you're doing Facebook, now is the
   time to start building that Page and
   looking for ways to get people to
   participate. Remember that marketing
   works best when you focus, and that
   doesn't just go for aspects of your
   campaign. You might sell a lot of
   different products or services, but it's
   best to pick just a few of them that sell
   well and have a broad appeal to your
   target market, and feature those in your
   advertising. Next, give some serious
   thought to what it is that you're selling.
   No, that doesn't mean your products or
   services. It means the *benefit* you're
   offering people. The solution to their
   problem, or the salve to their pain
   point. Remember the guy that buys a
   drill from the hardware store most likely
   does not want a drill, he just wants a

hole. Sell the hole or what your customer wants, not the drill. You need to appeal to people's emotions to get them to buy. If you're a novelist, you're not really selling a bunch of pieces of paper glued together with squiggly lines on them. You're selling engagement, excitement, enlightenment and emotion. If you are running a hair salon, you are not selling haircuts, you are selling beauty, self-confidence and emotional well-being. Figure out the emotional appeal of your products and services, then find out the words that will most relate to that emotional appeal. Use the words "You," and "Yours," never "Me," "My," "Our" or "We." Use emotional words with strong verbs – and always pair them with the keywords you're targeting through SEO or PPC (if applicable to your overall strategy, of course.) And never forget the power of coupons and offers! They are easy to track, have built-in urgency, and are devastatingly effective.

5. *Track and monitor your marketing efforts.* We'll go more into detail on this in the next (and final) chapter, but it's critical

that you know how your marketing is performing and react in a relevant (and rapid) manner. Which ads are performing, and where? Some ads will be effective on Google that won't work on Facebook, and vice-versa. Which ads *aren't* working? Those need to be replaced with others, or they need to be tweaked to see if you can wring more clicks out of them. Marketing is a constant process that requires experimentation, measurement and iteration; you never have any laurels to rest on, so get yourself into the habit of review and ad management early on.

Rating the Alternatives

Each of the alternatives presented in this book are effective in their own way, but different businesses will find varying levels of success depending on their marketing skill, individual character, effort put into it, and target audiences. Here is a list of all of the approaches in the book and a short assessment of the pros and cons of each.

Building a Website

There is no alternative to this if you are a business that caters to the public or commercial sector. Even if you go and register all of the listings at all of the review sites and establish an online presence that way. One of the few exceptions might be an individual or small firm that caters to clients by referral only, but then they should at least be using LinkedIn.

In order to engage in Internet marketing, you've got to build a functional, aesthetic Website you can direct customers to. It's the backbone of any online marketing campaign, and though it's one of the least expensive marketing methods out there, it's got one of the highest returns on investment.

If you're on a shoestring budget, you can start by using Tumblr or finding a service that will host your site for free, while publishing its own native advertising on your site. These aren't optimal options, because they detract from your business's credibility, but if it's the only way for you to get a website up and running, go ahead and get started. However, by using WordPress and a cheap hosting service (only at the start) you can usually get a basic, functional web page up and running with less than a day's work.

Search Engine Optimization

SEO works. Period. It is not dead as you may have heard and it is not even tired. You've got to do some basic SEO on your site – everyone does – no matter where you're focusing your efforts. You've got to do keyword research and assessment, no matter how tedious or bewildering it can seem at first, and spend your time making sure your tags and content are accessible to Google's bots. SEO is critical to ensuring that your website gets seen.

When we talk about SEO as a strategy, we're talking about a combination of content marketing and SEO techniques (although there is a form of content marketing that doesn't require a huge focus on SEO – more on that later.) That is, using regularly published content to ensure that your website continually ranks near the top of certain keyword searches. This usually means maintaining a blog that works within the post-Hummingbird Google parameters and consistently publishing frequently. This can be four to five times a week, if not every day, but could be less.

SEO is important for small businesses who are trying to reach a local audience, meaning within 30 miles of their location. It is even more necessary for businesses that are trying to reach a national or global audience.

An SEO strategy works best when paired with PPC, Facebook, and/or content marketing.

Paid Search

As mentioned in the chapter on PPC, this strategy is best used in concert with another strategy. If you're talking paid search, PPC is best with the SEO/blog or content marketing strategies. If you're talking PPC on Facebook, it of course works best with your other Facebook efforts and a Facebook-oriented content marketing strategy.

Please make note here that depending on your product or service PPC may be an excellent way to start and see relatively quick results. As stated earlier, it depends on your audience.

Content Marketing

By making your website the primary vehicle for content, you'll probably want to use SEO and PPC to augment your efforts. Content marketing doesn't make sense for everyone, however. If you're a business primarily focused on finding local foot traffic and not gunning for a wider, national or global audience, content marketing may prove to be too large of a waste of time and resources.

Before starting with content marketing, you also need to ask yourself whether you've got the chops to produce content of the quality you'll need to be successful. Creative writing is a skill few people have and even fewer people are expert in. Of course, anyone can write a blog, but high-quality, professional writing (that is also optimized for search) is a science and an art that usually takes a college degree to get started in – much less to get good at. If you did not major in English or you haven't had a natural proclivity toward writing your entire life, you may end up needing to hire a freelance writer. This can be a frustrating, difficult experience in and of itself if you end up struggling (like so many do) to find a professional on the marketplace who is both skilled, dependable, and reasonably priced. This is to say nothing of videos, images and InfoGraphics – those are just as difficult to produce, and often more expensive to hire professionals who can.

However, a content marketing approach to your Facebook efforts can yield huge results, again, depending on your audience. Content is the core of what gets shared on Facebook – not just text posts, but images, videos, InfoGraphics, articles and more. If you're trying to disseminate high-quality information to folks on Facebook to create engagement for your Page, it's important to create some of your own, of course. You can start with freelancers to create a small amount to put on your Page, for instance. But you'll also want to pass on other articles, white papers, images, videos and presentations you find around the Internet. Your audience will appreciate that you've put in time to curate content that's relevant to their interests, and it will help you build trust and goodwill among your potential customers. Just ensure that you're giving proper credit where it's due, and not plagiarizing others by failing to give a link to your sources.

Mobile Marketing

Mobile marketing is still cheaper than desktop Web advertising, but there is also a lower click through rate on mobile ads – and now you know why it's cheaper! Advertising with a mobile-optimized site works best with PPC practices, and getting signed up with ad networks. Of course, your mobile-optimized site needs to have the same level of basic SEO that your desktop site does, but for mobile customers who are on their phones, it's less common for them to read lengthy blogs or how-to articles. If you're trying a content marketing strategy in combination with mobile, you'll want to focus heavily on images and videos.

SMS marketing can be expensive, but you tend to get higher response rates than with traditional Email marketing, direct mail, telemarketing or mail. SMS makes sense for targeting consumers 18 through 55, although you'll get the best results from folks between 25 and 40. It also tends to be more effective for businesses that cater to specific, local regions, rather than Internet companies selling all over the country; thus, it's best paired up with strategies that optimize your local presence, such as a heavy focus on Google+ Business.

Author's note: We don't suggest SMS marketing at our firm unless we can identify a specific need. Based on current research it is one of the least trusted forms of marketing. This is just our opinion and it may be appropriate depending on the audience.

Facebook Marketing

Facebook marketing is relatively inexpensive, has a huge potential reach, and works for both brick-and-mortar and online companies. Though the non-ad part is free, it's very time-consuming, so if you are an owner/operator without a lot of extra time to pay attention to your Facebook Page and Groups, it can be hard to sustain over the long term.

Facebook ads can be very inexpensive when paired with solid demographic research and targeting. This components, actions, and metrics that make up a quality Facebook ad campaign would fill up another book. But things to remember are: 1) set a daily budget, 2) laser target your audience, 3) measure your results, 4) adjust and repeat. Facebook ads usually get old after just a few days and rarely are effective longer than a week.

Many businesses completely eschew marketing in other areas and focus only on Facebook. This is viable if you can prove a positive ROI, but like the other strategies, it works best in concert with another strategy. If you're looking to sell anywhere, try pairing it with an SEO/PPC campaign focused on your web page. If you're looking to sell locally, pair it with Google Business and mobile marketing.

Email Marketing

Email marketing is one of the oldest and remains one of the most cost effective online marketing channels I have seen. If done right, providing value, and with the recipient in mind should be included in every Internet marketing campaign you run. Always, always, always be building your Email list (or just your "list").

There is a saying in Internet marketing that "the money is in the list" and I believe this to be true. Whether on your website, your Facebook Page, your Google+ Business listing, at networking meetings, talking to prospective customers, anywhere, and everywhere; always collect Email addresses and add them to your list. One caveat; make sure you have permission before Emailing them. If they give you their Email then you do, I never use purchased lists.

Now start Emailing…

Google+ Business

There are almost no downsides to Google+ Business, unless you don't have a regular physical location. For instance, if you're one of the aforementioned freelance writers, or you primarily work in information without a steady office (besides home or the library) then it doesn't make sense to register your listing with Google+ Business. Google+ Business is best for businesses serving local areas, and can be an integral component of an online reputation management/cultivation strategy. It works well with any other strategy listed here, but it's best in concert with SMS marketing, reputation marketing and Facebook.

Author's note: In the right circumstances we believe a local marketing strategy that includes Google+ Business, an optimized website (on and off page), and Reputation Marketing is the most effective online marketing strategy available today. Plus if implemented correctly can have one of the highest ROIs of any strategy, tactic, or method. If you do nothing else for Internet Marketing then claim and optimize your Google+ Business page, do it today.

Your Online Reputation

This is Business 101 and possibly the most important method in this book: Your good name is all you have, so if you don't manage it carefully, you're liable to lose your entire business. This is especially important for businesses serving a particular region – you need to be aggressive and devout in your reputation monitoring and managing efforts. Like building a website, this is crucial for all businesses engaged in Internet marketing, and simply cannot be overlooked if you want any modicum of success in today's Brave New World.

Solutions: Keeping Track Of It All

In order to optimize your marketing efforts, you need to know how to track, measure and improve on what you're doing. *You cannot manage what you don't track.* If you're engaged in SEO, PPC, content marketing or social media marketing, Google or Facebook will provide some of the reporting and metrics – it's up to you to provide the analysis and judgment. If you're using SMS or Google+ Business as part of a concerted local effort, you'll get less in the way of metrics from external sources and will have to generate your own data to parse and learn from as you experiment with your marketing strategies.

Four Core Strategies to Measure Effectiveness

It's (almost) all about results. Of course, the most important number in all of your metrics is your Return on Investment – or ROI. How much business are you getting in return for the dollars you're plunking down on marketing? You're a small business, after all – creative or "brand" marketing is for players like Nike and Coca-Cola, but you've got to make sure every ad is filling your sales pipeline and demonstrating its worth to your company, or you won't be able to keep it in your budget.

But how do you know which of your campaigns are even effective in the first place? Here are four core strategies to use when ensuring you're getting the maximum ROI:

1. *Design a response-attribution scheme for all of your channels.* Marketing measurement isn't an afterthought – you have to plan for it ahead of time. Different channels need to be tracked in different ways (more on metrics in a moment.) You need to start with a goal and take incremental steps toward achieving that goal, or you'll end up scattershot and all over the map, without a clear measure of success. The question you need to be able to answer is: For a dollar spent on a particular channel are you able to trace revenue directly or indirectly related to that dollar spent? Set this up in advance and track it. Remember A/B or Split Testing?

2. *Create control groups.* If you're *really* small, you'll probably have to test your initial marketing on friends and family. But if you've got the resources, consider running a control group to collect data on the way people are responding to your marketing efforts and the way your campaign is "lifting."

3. *Your metrics are defined by your business's specific funnel.* With certain strategies, your metrics will be hand-delivered by Google or Facebook. But marketing is as much an art as it is a science, so you'll need to develop some of our own. For instance, if you sell big-ticket items, it's going to be just as important to qualify your leads as it is to make impressions with your advertisements. If you're in the business of making a larger quantity of smaller sales, it's going to be more important to encourage impulse and emotional buying. Whatever your funnel looks like, you'll need to develop metrics to see how well you're moving consumers through the process of becoming customers.

4. *Define specific attribution rules for each campaign.* Depending on your goals and the channel you're pursuing, you want to figure out the ways in which you'll track general customer response to each of your campaigns. You do need to differentiate these by campaign, because different target audiences and different tactics elicit unique responses, and you need to know which deserves the credit for increased sales, especially if they're cross-promoting.

The Basic Metrics

Figuring out customer response isn't an easy thing to do, but there are certain, tested methods that can help you get on the right track. Here are the five basic metrics involved with measuring Internet marketing success:

1. *Money spent.* This is pretty easy – it's the amount of money you've spent on your campaign to this point. This functions as the baseline for many of the other metrics.

2. *Impression.* An "impression" occurs whenever your ad pops up in front of someone. It's tempting to think of this

as the number of people who have *seen* your ad, but this isn't necessarily the case. It's better to think of it as the number of people to whom your ad has been made available, because many folks' eyes tend to glaze over whenever an advertisement enters their field of vision. Unfortunately, this is due to marketing fatigue, and there isn't a lot you, as a small business, can do about that, except to be as creative as possible with advertisements to try and get folks to give your business a second look. Stay within an advertiser's Terms of Service but be BOLD. Use colors and other components that contrast with the page your ads display on. For example Red on Facebook is popular because of the white and blue colors that dominate pages on Facebook. If they don't see it then they don't see it.

3. *Click.* A "click" occurs whenever someone, well, clicks on your ad to go to your landing page, Google+ Business listing, Facebook Page, or wherever you send them.   To get shortened versions of links that work well and don't take up a lot of space just head over to Google's

links shortening service at goo.gl, tinyURL.com, or Bitly.com. One note: Many marketers conflate "click" with "likes" and "shares" on Facebook, because they denote engagement. Essentially, a click is the qualification of a lead, separating people who are interested (but not necessarily ready to buy) from the general populace. For ads on Facebook a "click" and a "Like" can be the same thing depending on how you set up your ad.

4. *Conversion.* A "conversion" occurs when someone takes action from your landing page. This means something different for every strategy. Maybe someone searched a keyword, saw your ad, clicked through to your page and then responded to your call-to-action in some way. Maybe they "Liked" something on Facebook, or showed up in the store after receiving a text message. You have to determine what success looks like here. Is it sales orders? Capturing their Email address on an opt-in page or box? New subscriptions to your newsletter? Downloads of your e-book? If you're

using PPC, when you set up your AdWords account, you put a little bit of tracking code on your website that tells Google whenever someone has converted, and they keep track of those conversions for you. Otherwise, you'll have to develop ways to help you tally these.

5. *Return on Investment.* As mentioned before, this is far and away the most important metric, but it's also the least useful for refining your marketing strategy. To calculate your return on investment, you have to figure out how much money you've made as a result of your marketing efforts (usually by tracking converted sales) and divide that by the amount of money you've spent thus far.

The Advanced Metrics

Of course, the five basic metrics are incredibly important to track, but there are others you need to keep an eye on, as well. These we are calling the "advanced metrics" and they are actually extensions of the basic metrics. There are four advanced metrics:

1. *Click Through Rate (CTR.)* This is the percentage of impressions that become clicks, "likes," "shares" or other lead qualifications. This is a percentage metric, so you want it to be as high as you can get it. CTR measures the efficiency of your Internet marketing campaign, and you can derive it by dividing your clicks by your impressions. A good CTR depends on different factors but for Google AdWords 1% to 3% may be considered very good.

2. *Conversion Rate.* This is the percentage of clicks that become conversions. This is also a percentage metric, so you want it to be high. Conversion Rate, like CTR, measures the efficiency of your campaign (and the effectiveness of your landing page.) You can derive it by dividing your conversions by your clicks. This can vary widely depending on the campaign. Sometimes 3% will be consider good while other times 10% will be considered low. It depends on your sales funnel, how well you have qualified your leads by the time they get to your call to action. We know of one

campaign and sales funnel that had over a 90% Conversion Rate, but their leads were super qualified and by the time the lead reached the call to action they had essentially already bought.

3. *Cost Per Click (CPC.)* This is the dollar amount that you spend on each click. It's your cost metric, so you of course want to get it as low as possible without sacrificing delivery on the other metrics. You can derive CPC by dividing your money spent by your clicks. In Google AdWords you will get lots of help to increase your CPC, be cautious. Look at your keywords, your competition, your gross revenue on a conversion and decide when you can increase your bids and when you may want to fold or not raise your bid. Chasing the best keyword may have a low or even negative ROI while going after the second or third best keyword may be more efficient.

4. *Cost Per Acquisition (CPA.)* This is the dollar amount that you spend on each conversion. Like CPC, it's a cost metric, so you want to keep this low.

You can derive CPA by dividing your money spent by your conversions. Keep in mind a conversion may not be a sale but could be acquiring an Email address, phone number, etc.

A simple rule of thumb: Keep your percentage metrics high and your cost metrics low, and you'll have an efficient campaign. It's a good idea to set goals for your campaign's performance in each of these metrics, and then work to optimize and refine your strategies until you reach them.

Other Metrics

Here are some other common metrics small businesses use to track their Internet Marketing efforts:

1. *Email opens.* If you decide to embark on an Email campaign (and you should), you want to know how many people are actually opening the Emails you send out. This is similar to the "impressions" metric explained above.

2. *Email clicks.* All modern Email service providers track who clicked on what link in your Email and how many times. Include multiple links to the same

destination with variations in the hypertext (the text in front of the link) to see which variations and placements have the highest number of clicks. Then in future Emails use the link hypertext and placement that had the most clicks. Keep testing and refining.

3. *Form conversion rate.* If your landing page asks people to fill out a contact form (usually in exchange for a coupon, or for content of some kind) you'll want to know how many people actually finished the process of completing the form. Form conversion rate helps you understand how many leads you're generating, but it won't give you any insight into how your marketing campaign is affecting your revenue.

4. *Customer Acquisition Cost (CAC.)* This is the total of your sales and marketing efforts. Basically, how much money does it cost in advertising to bring someone out of the blue and convert them into a paying customer? We think this is huge at our firm and a crucial metric to help you determine how much you can or should be spending on your

Internet marketing. For example if you are a car repair shop and let's say each new customer spends an average of $750 with a 33% gross margin. And let's say you are spending $1,000 per month on Internet marketing. Then you would need about 4 new customers per month to break even ($750 x .33 x 4). Keep in mind this example is not considering the lifetime or even yearly value of a customer which should be included in the calculation but was not for simplicity.

5. *Lifetime Value (LTV.)* Lifetime value is how much a customer is worth to you over the life of that customer patronizing your business. This is crucial for small businesses that depend on a recurring revenue stream from their customers. We also suggest considering the Annual Value of a customer for budgeting and planning.

The Wrap

You've arrived at the end of the book, and you now have a comprehensive understanding of Internet marketing for small business. As always, it's up to you to make the most of the knowledge you've gained. The most important thing to realize about marketing is that in order to be good at it, you'll have to find within you a writer's touch, a salesperson's savvy and a hustler's musical energy. The whole point of this practice is not only to move your business forward in the sometimes bewildering Digital Age, but to create and retain new customers that will create a sustainable business that will provide for you and your family over the long term.

You've learned the different alternative forms of Internet marketing, the synergy between them, and gotten some advice on which kinds of business will thrive with which strategies. You've learned the importance of Google and Facebook, the power of paid search and SEO, and received tips and tricks on how to reach customers busily on the go with no computer in sight but the smartphone in their pocket. You've also learned how to plan an Internet marketing strategy, and how to track and measure the effectiveness of your efforts.

Now you're ready to get out there and put your knowledge to work. Experience is the best teacher, after all. The most important thing you can do is to start; the second most important is to keep going.

In closing if you have any questions, suggestions, or comments about this book, it's contents, or us here at www.mediamarketexperts.com please do not hesitate to contact us at service@mediamarketexperts.com.

Best Wishes and Good Luck!

Index

195